MW00808017

Most people feel overwl
family and parenting cai. ____ __. _____ __mpetition to the
time and demands of career and work-life. I have watched
many people lose their way from this pressure. What Russell
offers within the pages of *In Search of Work-Life Balance* is a
practical way of seeing this problem and an achievable way
for bringing a God-honoring, family-strengthening solution
into reality. Not only have I listened to him teach these
principles, I have had the privilege of watching him live them.
I am confident this book will make a significant difference
within both your family and career.

Joel Eason, Senior Pastor, Bridgeway Church

Full of practical and faith-based strategies for finding your
life-work rhythm, Russell's book is small in size but big on
ideas. A must-read for everyone from the empty nest
executive, to the mid-life middle manager, to the recent
college graduate starting his or her career.

Chad Gibbs, author of *God & Football: Faith and
Fanaticism in the SEC*

The bookstores of America are littered with faith-based books
on success in one form or another. Dr. Clayton's book *In
Search of Work-Life Balance*, however, stands out in a
crowded field. By using a common sense approach to
obtaining a healthy work-life balance, this book will give you
the tools to make a positive change in your life. Add this book
to your success library and share it with your friends.

Guy Fawkes, Owner, VoIPWRX Telecommunications

This struggle with work-life balance is something that we can
really relate to, as it was a constant struggle for our entire
professional career. Russell has hit a home run in this book
by combining well-documented research with real examples
and the truths of Scripture. He offers a down-to-earth and
practical approach to this problem that is plaguing our
culture, and the helpful action points make it easy to see how
we can apply the principles to our lives. If you struggle with
maintaining a healthy work-life balance, we highly
recommend this quick, helpful book and encourage you to
take it to heart.

Drs. Richard and Celia Thompson, Founders / Owners,
Tavares Animal Hospital (retired after 34 years)

As a busy mom and business owner, I loved how practical and to-the-point the book was. I was able to finish it quickly and find useful tips that also tied in biblical examples. I have never read a book that included all of these main points together, and I found them all refreshing and important. As a result of reading *In Search of Work-Life Balance*, I have already put several of the strategies into practice and will continue to be more in-tuned to my work-life balance as a result of the helpful content of this book.

Karen Green, Owner, The Reading Corner

Russell does a great job of integrating faith and everyday living. Every working person struggles at times to strike the balance between hard work and responsible family time. Clayton's *In Search of Work-Life Balance* shares Biblical truth and practical advice about life and work that can help any person be successful in both.

Cliff Knight, Associate Pastor, Minister to Families, Lakeview Baptist Church

In our culture, it is so easy to get caught up in a sort of "work martyr" mentality, where your identity comes out of how long and hard you work, and family easily gets put on the back burner. *In Search of Work-Life Balance* challenges us to step away from this new (non-Biblical) norm, and completely shift our goals to obtain a balanced, Godly life. Russell's book has challenged me to be a better wife, mother, and employee, while giving practical, obtainable ideas as to subtle lifestyle changes that will make a huge impact.

Jessica Aviles, Director of Growth Groups, Bridgeway Church

In Search of
Work-Life
BALANCE

In Search of *Work-Life* BALANCE

*A Small Book with a Faith-Based
Approach to a Large Problem*

Russell Clayton, Ph.D.

Clayton, Russell
In Search of Work-Life Balance: A Small Book with a Faith-Based Approach to a Large Problem
ISBN-13: 978-0692806920 (softcover)

Editor: Blake Atwood
Cover Design: Anthony Guagliardo, Armored Rooster Studios
Interior Design: Alicia Clayton
Author Photo: Dani Adams, DigitalMyst Photography

For Alicia, Emily, and Elizabeth,
you are truly a blessing.

For Mom, Dad, and Kelly,
thank you for being a great example
of family from the very beginning.

CONTENTS

INTRODUCTION

Andrea is a successful, married lawyer in her mid-thirties with two children. She's also a chronic Facebook user. Earlier this year, she posted,

"Ugh!!! Here I am again...it's 10 o'clock and I'm still in my office working...and haven't seen my kids all day! Is this what 'adulting' is supposed to look like? #Imissmykids"

Andrea's job, along with her husband's, provides the family with a comfortable living, including nice cars, trendy clothes, and a house in the *it* neighborhood. This sounds like the life, right? But Andrea frequently posts messages like these on social media sites, and two common threads have emerged in her postings:

1) She openly grumbles about how she's in the office working late (and missing her children).
2) She gushes over the time she spends with her children and husband (while also noting that it's the first time she's seen them in three or four days).

Billable hours define success in her line of work, and billable hours often mean being in an office and not at home.

Andrea has a life many of us would characterize as lacking "work-life balance" because she works long hours and is often away from her loved ones. While I don't have the ability to read her mind, her social media posts indicate regret over not getting to spend enough time at home with her family. And it's not just Andrea. I see this same type of post from men and women to whom I'm connected across multiple social media platforms. Truth be told, many of us have felt like Andrea, perhaps not on a daily basis, but more often than we'd like.

A tension undoubtedly exists between our workplaces and our homes. Our bosses, customers, and coworkers want us to be constantly available and work longer hours, both at the workplace and sometimes from home. On the other hand, our spouses and children are just as demanding of our time and attention—and rightfully so. A late-night strategizing session at the office interferes with your child's school play that same evening. Working on the weekend to impress the boss and hopefully secure a promotion leaves your spouse alone on a Saturday. Scenarios like these are all too common.

A recent Gallup Poll revealed that 21 percent of Americans work between fifty to fifty-nine hours each week and another 18 percent work more than sixty hours each week.[1] This means two in every five Americans are working more than fifty hours per week. We shouldn't be surprised when research studies[2] show that longer working hours are linked to work-life *im*balance and stress-related health and psychological problems.

Work-life balance is a buzzword in offices across the U.S. and in popular business publications such as *Forbes* and the *Harvard Business Review*. Many of us seek work-life balance but do *not* actually have this ever-elusive balance between our work and home lives. On the other hand, a lot of information is also encouraging us to push harder, dream bigger, and accumulate more stuff. There's nothing inherently wrong with "going hard" at the workplace, having dreams about what you'd like life to look like, and having a nice house and stylish clothes. But do those desires come at the expense of neglecting a spouse or children?

Some people might wonder, "Do I really need work-life balance?" After all, many people find a lot of satisfaction in being successful in the marketplace, even if this success comes with spending many hours at the office. These individuals might not put in as many hours at home as their spouse or children might like, but at least they're making money and providing for their family. Isn't that in and of itself a noble calling?

Furthermore, does God truly care if we live a life where work and home are balanced? Isn't He more concerned about hot-button issues such as abortion, sex-trafficking, and illicit drug use? And can there really be "balance" between these two roles of work and non-work? How will we provide for our families if we're not fulfilling our obligations as an employee to our respective industries and employers? What if we looked at these questions from a biblical perspective? Would this adjust our view on work-life balance? Would we shift our priorities a bit?

Join me in discovering what God has to say about managing the intersection of work and family (Spoiler alert: He's in favor of work-life balance!). Suppose you don't need convincing of the importance of work-life balance; rather, you want to know *how* to attain it. We'll explore many practical steps so you can better manage the interplay between work and life, including some of today's best practices used by successful individuals and families. Additionally, the practical advice presented in this book has undergone both personal testing and is supported by years of research, including hundreds of researchers and thousands of research participants.

This work-life issue fascinates me because I find myself right smack in the middle of it as a husband and father. I've spent the majority of my academic career researching work-life balance and have published my research in well-respected academic journals. My research has also been mentioned by popular press outlets such as *Harvard Business Review*, *NBC News*, and *USA Today*, to name a few. And not only do I conduct my own research on work-life balance because I actually like this stuff and think it's fascinating, but I spend time staying up-to-date on the latest findings from other top researchers in the area who study why and how people achieve what they love doing but also long to spend time with those important to them. *

Due to my experiences of trying to prioritize work-life balance, I wrote this book for several reasons:

1) The topic is relevant to many adults.
2) My research focuses on the topic.
3) I wanted to add a Christian perspective to the topic.

The goal of this book is not to bore you to death with tons of academic studies. Quite the contrary: the purpose is to give you a list of practical steps to implement immediately. And it just so happens that these steps are based on scientific research that has been proven to make a difference and impact lives for the better. †

The first chapter will discuss why work-life balance is an issue that has a spiritual basis behind it and how a faith-based approach can aid us in finding an appropriate balance. The chapters that follow will outline ways we can begin to create balance in our lives, complete with action steps in each chapter. Chapter 2 will discuss how our daily walk with God is the foundation for work-life balance. This practical advice is the only non-negotiable in the book. We must consistently align our priorities with God, or we run the risk of putting other priorities before His

---

* You're probably forming a pretty nerdy impression of me at this point—but wait! Keep reading!

† I've read the boring academic studies so that you don't have to!

purpose for us. The chapters that follow can then be treated like a smorgasbord of strategies for work-life balance.

While ultimately I would like for you to work all of the tips from each chapter into your life, you could pick three or four to start with and add additional tips into your routine over time. Perhaps you may start by adding exercise into your weekly schedule (Chapter 3) along with working to increase your emotional intelligence (Chapter 4). Once you have a good grasp on those and see how they're positively impacting your work-life balance, you might then begin to utilize the time management practices in Chapter 5 and so on.

Join me as we look at what the Bible says about pursuing work-life balance. Then I'll let you in on some of the best ways to achieve work-life balance. Let's get started!

1

A FAITH-BASED PERSPECTIVE FOR WORK-LIFE BALANCE

As I mentioned in the introduction, I wanted to write this book in part because there are only a handful of books on this topic specifically for Christians. Before we dig in, let's get some housekeeping out of the way:

1) The term "work-life balance" is *not* a great way to talk about the intersection of work and family. Balance implies that an equal amount of time will be spent physically and mentally at work and at home. Rarely, if ever, do we spend an even twelve hours each day at the office and another twelve hours at home (or with our family). A better way to look at this concept is effective work-life integration, or finding your rhythm between work and life.

That said, the term work-life balance is so common to our culture's vocabulary that we'll go with it for the purposes of this book. Switching up the terminology from work-life balance to work-life fill-in-the-blank would be like asking you to stop saying "ice cream" in favor of saying "frozen concoction made of milk and sugar." It just wouldn't work well. So when I say "work-life balance," I'm referring to the idea of *juggling the prioritized areas of our lives for maximum efficiency in the areas of work and family*. Said another way, work-life balance refers to "finding the peace of God that governs our conscience to A) balance working hard, B) lead our family faithfully, and C) rest enough to take care of God's temple (i.e., our body)."[1]

2) The term "work" does not have to be limited to the traditional idea of working from 8:00 a.m. to 5:00 p.m. at an office. Being a stay-at-home parent can be just as much *work* as it is *family*. Managing a household is similar to being the project manager at a job site. It's easy for us to get caught up in creating efficiency and effectiveness in this role. And it's easy for us to slip into the household role of "boss" instead of "mom" or "dad" due to the demands of being a stay-at-home parent. Additionally, work doesn't even have to refer to paid employment as the traditional sense of the word implies. Volunteering at a church or nonprofit organization can be just as demanding of a job as one where earning a wage is involved.

Furthermore, the term "work" does not have to have a negative overtone to it. Many times the mention of work can invoke less-than-happy thoughts, particularly if we do not enjoy our jobs. However, the Bible clearly states that working is part of God's plan, with God putting Adam to work taking care of the garden of Eden in Genesis 2.

3) We have seasons in life when our time at work far outweighs our time with family. These seasons are inevitable and may not be indicative of a significant work-life *im*balance. If you're a tax accountant, then your work schedule is probably very hectic from January 1 until April 15 each year. Or perhaps you're a schoolteacher directing the school play. You're likely to have some late nights building stage sets and conducting rehearsals for several weeks leading up to the show.

As a college professor I have a few seasons where my job requires a lot of attention, and so much so that it takes me away from home more than I'd like for a few days each semester. In particular, the end of each semester is filled with final exams to give, papers to grade, and deadlines for when grades must be posted. Writing this book is another one of those seasons. In fact, as I type

> **As Christ-followers our faith should underpin everything we do.**

this sentence it is 8:52 on a Friday night, and I'm still at the office (by choice) writing this chapter. And this is with the support and approval of my wife. However, I also spent an entire workday earlier this week at home (by choice) watching cartoons and playing "Chase Emmy!" with my daughter. The key to these examples is that this *im*balance exists only for a season, is strategic in nature, and is *not* a habitual way of life.

4) As Christ-followers our faith should underpin everything we do. This is a tall task, but one to which we are called. Colossians 3:23 says that we are to work as working unto the Lord. As such, our roles of employee, boss, spouse, and/or parent must be guided by biblical principles.

Now that we're all on the same page, let's look at this idea of work-life balance from a biblical standpoint.

Does God Care about Work-Life Balance?

It's Not Like It's a Big Sin

If you've been a Christ-follower for very long at all, then you know we tend to beat the drum loudly and emphatically against the "big" sins such as adultery and abortion, and rightfully so, as these sins bring with them severe repercussions for those involved. On the other hand, we tend to sweep other issues under the rug or simply look the other way. We think to ourselves, "I may be doing such-and-such, but at least I'm not like *him*," and that provides us with a little comfort. Let's put this into the context of work-life balance.

To be clear, I am *not* claiming that work-life *im*balance is a sin. But what if some of the underlying root causes of *im*balance are sinful? As my friend Solomon Kafoure, a small business owner and father of three in Nashville, puts it, we're dealing with a "*root* issue versus a *fruit* issue." That is, working an average of twelve hours per day is not the *root,* or the actual sin, but rather the *fruit* (outward sign) of a sin. Let me

20

dig in a little deeper there. There is nothing sinful about working twelve hours per day. The number of hours we work is itself *not* a sin. However, it may be the fruit, or outward sign, of the underlying sin. The root is the sin. And the sin might be coveting a material possession to the point that we will do almost whatever it takes to get it.

In *Respectable Sins*, Jerry Bridges points out several "small" sins, such as selfishness and discontentment, all of which are typically viewed as acceptable in the modern church. Here's an example: if I were physically abusive to my wife, several of our church friends would call me to the carpet on it (and probably have me arrested). That's a "big" sin and is generally not tolerated in our society, much less among the body of Christ-followers. On the other hand, I've had conversations in which I've expressed my disgust with my slow, older-model iPhone, and these conversations have taken place within the walls of a church building. But no one has ever called me out on expressing my discontentment with my iPhone, car, or computer. Instead, we call this a "first-world problem" and laugh it off.

So how does this all relate to work-life balance? I can't help but wonder if some of these "respectable sins" aren't at the root of our culture's proclivity to work so much, leading to a disparity between the amount of time we spend at work versus with our family. Perhaps we are so selfish that we'd rather stay at work than come home and help with a chore or project that we're not interested in. Or maybe we work long hours because we get a rush from excelling at our job. In either case, we are putting our needs ahead of those at home. This selfish behavior is discussed in God's Word. We find in Philippians 2:3–4 that we should "Do nothing from selfishness or empty conceit, but with humility of mind regard one another as more important than yourselves; do not merely look out for your personal interests, but also for the interests of others." So should I stay an extra two and a half hours at the office or go help out at home?

As I mentioned earlier, we all have seasons of life during which that extra time may be absolutely crucial to the proper functioning of the workplace. These scenarios are almost unavoidable from time-to-time. However, if I choose to stay late at work to avoid going home to help with dinner and putting my children to bed, then I am guilty of selfishness. The choices we all have to make about our work-life balance most definitely contain a spiritual component.

Part of my job as a college professor is certainly to teach classes and advise students. But another significant part of being a professor is to conduct research.* While classes are taught within a defined period during the semester, research can take place at any time. I am often tempted to stay late and work on research because I truly enjoy it. However, this would come at the expense of spending time with my wife and daughters. If I consistently stayed at my office to work on research instead of coming home, I would effectively be saying, "My time is more important

---

* I'll share some of my research with you in subsequent chapters—it's not as boring as it sounds!

than yours, and I'd rather work on my research than spend it with you." So, is my ambition to publish another academic article a sin? Not really. There is nothing fundamentally wrong with publishing a research study. But if my interest in publishing another research study causes me to neglect my family constantly, then I have to believe God is not happy with that.

Maybe your selfish act at work involves the thrill of the hunt, such as securing that new client or closing the big deal, which takes you away too many nights during the week, entertaining clients over dinner or at sporting events. Again, there's nothing wrong with trying to gain an account or make a sale, but if this ambition consistently keeps you from being an active participant in your family's life in favor of being with clients, this may indicate a selfish attitude at the root of your *im*balance. Those of you who have jobs with non-traditional working hours may be thinking, "This guy's giving me a hard time because I'm not home for family dinner, but my normal work hours are during dinner!" The point I'm trying to make is that it's okay to miss a family event from time to time. However, consistently missing out on family time should not be the norm.

The traditional working hours of 8:00 a.m. to 5:00 p.m. do not apply to many jobs. Some people work jobs where they are seven days on and seven days off instead of the traditional Monday-to-Friday schedule. There's nothing inherently wrong with that. The same principles can apply to such non-traditional jobs. A great example of this is my neighbor Skip Cordrey.

He works as an air traffic controller and has a revolving schedule. He goes in to work at 7:00 a.m. on some days, and on other days he doesn't go in until 6:30 p.m. While his non-traditional working hours are sure to cause him to miss certain family events, which is unavoidable due to his line of work, he is fully devoted and available to his wife and children during his time off.

Our selfishness is not limited to the workplace but can also extend to our hobbies. Many years ago as a single college student, I went out on a date with a young lady. During our date, she asked a simple question: "Do you play golf?" As it turns out, I am not much of a golfer, so I told her no. My initial thought was that she was really into golf and wanted to talk about golf or go play a round. However, after asking the question she proceeded to explain to me how golf had led to her parents' divorce and a severely fractured relationship between her and her father. Her dad had literally played so much golf that he was never available for his wife and daughter.

Golf is not a bad hobby. Neither is exercising, building model trains, or scrapbooking. However, a good hobby can become bad when it leads to the negligence of our family (or work for that matter). Regardless of what causes us to act selfishly to the detriment of our family, it should be noted that Galatians 5:20 lists "selfish ambition" as an act of the flesh, along with the likes of debauchery and drunkenness.[†] That's a tough pill to swallow!

[†] NIV

Respectable Sins also lists discontentment and worldliness as sins that are seen as acceptable, and I believe these too can be at the root of work-life *im*balance. Bridges primarily focuses his discussion of discontentment on the "painful circumstances of life," such as physical disabilities. However, I believe the trivial causes of much of our discontentment can give way to worldliness and materialistic desires. ‡

Bridges uses 1 Corinthians to define worldliness as "being attached to, engrossed in, or preoccupied with the things of this temporal life." What a great definition! Am I so preoccupied with making enough money so that I can take an exotic vacation that I routinely put in eighty-hour workweeks? If so, this is likely an unhealthy pattern that points to a worldly perspective. There's nothing wrong with a vacation. In fact, I believe routine vacations are a great way to spend time with your family.§ Over the past year, my family has taken short getaways to Walt Disney World and the beautiful Gulf Coast beaches of Florida. However, these trips were done in a cost-effective manner and were financed within the scope of our normal budget without me or my wife having to work excessively to make these short trips possible.

Maybe the vacation isn't the reason you're working long hours. Maybe you're looking to get a big house in the *it* neighborhood or to drive the expensive luxury car you've always wanted. Houses and cars take money. And those things are not particularly

---

‡ Like my old iPhone taking seven seconds to launch an app instead of two seconds like the newer model.
§ Or even just you and your spouse: leave the kids with grandma!

wrong on the surface. It's okay to have a nice home. I've heard many people say, "Money is the root of all evil" as a way to justify *not* having nice houses or cars, but that's not exactly accurate. First Timothy 6:10 tells us, "For the *love* of money is a root of all sorts of evil" (emphasis added). God is okay with us having a desire to make money. In fact, He wants us to work so that we can provide for ourselves (2 Thessalonians 3:10–12) and others (Ephesians 4:8). But when worldliness gives way to the love of money to fund materialistic desires, we run the risk of working too many hours too often in an effort to pay for such a lifestyle. And we find in 1 John 2 that we should "not love the world nor the things in the world"[15] and that "the world is passing away."[17]

> *An imbalance as a result of chasing the desires of the world is an outward reflection of an inward issue.*

An *im*balance as a result of chasing the desires of the world is an outward reflection of an inward issue. So it may be that our selfishness, discontentment, or materialism is being made visible by our *im*balance between work and family. Getting to the heart and soul of the root issue will help us find a better balance.

So I'm a Workaholic! Isn't that Better than Being Lazy?

A common line of reasoning for working too much, especially by men, goes like this: "So I'm working a lot, and I'm away from home . . . but it's okay because I'm making money and providing my family with the means to do what we all desire to do." Providing for our families is a noble calling. After all, as I noted earlier, 1 Timothy 5:8 instructs us to provide for our household. In addition, we tend to justify working long hours by comparing ourselves, as hard-working, productive members of society, to those who do not work to provide for their families. While this is not a great argument in favor of workaholism, God's Word does speak against being a lazy sluggard.

Many of the Proverbs warn against laziness. For example, in the description of a woman of noble character, Proverbs 31:27 notes that such a woman does not "eat the bread of idleness." The way of the lazy is also compared to a path full of thorns and briers (Proverbs 15:19). And Proverbs 21:25 warns that the desire of the sluggard will kill him because he does not work. The effect of a lazy sluggard on another person is even equated to the unpleasant sensation of smoke getting into one's eyes (ouch!) (Proverbs 10:26). The New Testament notes: "For even when we were with you, we used to give you this order: if anyone is not willing to work, then he is not to eat, either. For we hear that some among you are leading an undisciplined life, doing no work at all, but acting like busybodies" (2 Thessalonians 3:10–11).

This biblical evidence is enough to warrant the conclusion that God does *not* want us to be habitually lazy. So does this mean that just being a hard worker is justified? And, if so, does that give us license to put in endless hours at the workplace, at a volunteer position we hold, or in a hobby? Not exactly.

I believe God cares deeply about our work. He tells us in Ephesians 4:28 that we should labor and do honest work. In Ecclesiastes 9:10, He commands us to work "with all [our] might," which indicates that we should have a strong work ethic. However, while we are instructed to not be a lazy sluggard, nowhere in the Bible are we commanded (or given permission) to make working long hours a habitual way of life. That said, many of us are tempted to put in too many hours at work to the neglect of our home life, Christians included. And we do this under the guise of "providing for my family." I do not believe God is honored by that. Why? Because God has given us instructions to make our spouse a priority (e.g., Genesis 2:24) and to raise our children in a godly home (e.g., Deuteronomy 6:6–7). At the most basic level, these two instructions are hard to accomplish if we are at the worksite for too many hours and away from home on a regular basis.

As noted at the onset of this chapter, we are certainly all going to have seasons in which we must work harder and put in longer hours than normal. And this is okay. I am not advocating for us to all work the traditional forty-hour workweek and nothing more. We have seasons when our work requires more than this. The idea of seasons in life is

28

biblical. Ecclesiastes 3 tells us, "There is an appointed time for everything. And there is a time for every event under heaven." Said another way, the circumstances in which we live are constantly changing and require an appropriate response.

I love how my friend Tim Harris, a senior technology consultant, puts it: "Doing quality work means that at times, for relatively short durations, work will demand above-normal focus, energy, and time commitment." The key phrase here is *short durations* of time. Tim is not putting in seventy-hour workweeks on a regular basis. Doing so would violate his convictions and would take him away from his wife and kids more than he'd like. But as a business professional, he recognizes that doing quality work may have its seasons when more is demanded of him. So how do we quantify a "short duration of time" and apply that to our lives? I truly believe this will be based on us having a spirit of discernment and listening to the guidance of the Holy Spirit (You'll read more on this in Chapter 2, and see John 14:16–17.)

Finding the "Balance"

So we've established that God does not want us consistently overworking and that He does not want us to be a lazy sluggard. So how can we find the middle ground? Using the definition from earlier in this chapter, how can we effectively A) balance working hard, B) lead our family faithfully, and C) rest enough to take care of God's temple?

In the chapters that follow, I will discuss seven concepts that can assist us in our efforts to balance work with family. Each of these concepts has been researched by social scientists, supporting their usefulness in our daily lives. The first concept we will discuss is the idea of a consistent walk with God, or what I will refer to as our "spiritual well-being." As noted earlier, the other chapters that follow may be treated like a cafeteria-line approach ("I'll have some of this, but pass on that"), but the next chapter is non-negotiable. That is, putting the subsequent chapters and their concepts into practice will be futile without first focusing on your walk with God.

2

SPIRITUAL WELL-BEING

*The most important thing you bring to your family
is a healthy soul.*
— Joel Eason, Pastor, Bridgeway Church

We established in the preceding pages that God *does* care about our work-life balance. This makes God a great place to start, as He is an incredible resource at our disposal when we seek to balance work and family. Asking God to help us with our work-life balance may sound a bit trivial, like asking Him to provide us with a parking space at a crowded shopping mall during the Christmas shopping season. But I believe this is the best way for us to align our work and family priorities with His priorities, leading to a better balance between work and life.

My friend Ryan is a husband and father of four daughters along with being the pastor of a thriving church. His situation is the perfect recipe for a busy life. Most pastors are stretched thin and have a lot of demands placed on them by their congregations.* It would be very easy for him to work fourteen-hour days preparing sermons, visiting church members in the hospital, attending community events, and serving his congregation. It's for this reason that Ryan told me he prays each morning, "Lord, transform me and make me by your Word and your Spirit to be the kind of husband, father, and pastor that I need to be today. It's not really about me." This is a basic prayer, but it's also a beautiful example of how we should call upon the Lord to help us with work-life balance, no matter our profession.

Perhaps you're not a pastor or parent of four children. Maybe you're a husband, a father of one, and an accountant, or maybe you're a wife and a teacher with two kids at home. Either way, your life can get just as busy as people in other professions and with other demands. At a men's retreat, my pastor commented, "The most important thing you bring to your family is a healthy soul." I believe that statement is incredibly compelling. After all, if my soul isn't healthy, how am I going to have a healthy relationship with my wife and daughters? Attending to our spiritual well-being is important so that we're able to achieve better work-life balance.

Spiritual well-being refers to whether we are consistently seeking God's will for our lives, praying, and spending time reading the Bible. So a person who routinely does those three activities would be considered to have high spiritual well-being. In

---

* Just ask your pastor!

contrast, a person who rarely prays and spends time in the Bible would be low in spiritual well-being. Praying and reading the Bible are tenets of our faith and are found in most Christian living books on the market. So how are they applied to work-life balance? You likely know that praying and reading the Bible are common Christian practices, but how exactly is spiritual well-being connected to the issue of work-life balance?

I believe seeking God helps us balance work and life in two interconnected ways:

1) by aligning our priorities with His, and
2) by decreasing our selfishness in favor of being self*less* to our family.

My Priorities

I remember as a college student making many plans for my future. Most of these plans revolved around what I wanted my career to look like, and I'm pretty sure that my plans changed about twenty times between my freshman year and graduation. I wanted to be everything from a general manager of a professional sports team to the top marketing guy in an advertising agency. And, like many of us, a lot of my career planning centered around, "How much money can I make in this job, or that job?" Looking back, I rarely consulted with God about the direction He wanted my career to go. Instead, I dreamed of having jobs with prestigious titles and big paychecks. Keep in mind there's nothing wrong with making money and having fancy job titles. I know several people who have both and also manage to make family a top priority. However, throughout college on up until I was five years into my career, I did not actively seek God's will for my career. Rather, I chased a bigger paycheck from one organization to the next. My priority was to advance through the job ranks and make more money, rarely seeking God's plan for my life, which led to quite a bit of job-related stress.

His Priorities

Fast-forward to today, where I have a job that allows me to invest significant amounts of time in my family. I didn't just stumble into this career. It wasn't until I began to seek God's will that He showed me the plans he had for my career and the path He wanted me to travel to get to where I am now. In fact, His plan for me required that I quit a salaried job in order to go back to graduate school full-time. Let me say that again: I quit a full-time salaried position in order to go back to graduate school for four years. That's not something I would have done without assurance from God.

His assurance was not that He would give my family so many thousands of dollars to live on each year and to get me through graduate school in so many years. Rather, my wife and I leaned on God's assurance in Matthew 6:33: "But seek first His kingdom and His righteousness, and all these things will be added to you." Because we were seeking God, we were able to have faith that His plan was the best plan for us. My natural inclination would have been to keep my salaried job because that was how I made money. However, aligning my priorities with God made all the difference in where my career is now and my ability to balance work and family.

Now that I have the career I believe God called me to, I am far less stressed at my job and have many opportunities to spend time with my family. Sure, my job has its own "busy seasons" as I mentioned earlier; however, I am more fulfilled at work and at home knowing I have been obedient to His calling.

> *I am more fulfilled at work and at home knowing I have been obedient to His calling.*

Praying is a great way to seek God and to be in His presence, and my wife and I certainly did a lot of praying while trying to discern God's will for my career. However, another great way to align with God is through the reading of Scripture. My personal preference is to read the Bible for a few minutes in the morning as a way to center myself with God. This might be a chapter from Proverbs or a short passage from the New Testament. In any case, doing this helps me to frame my day and reminds me that it's not all about me.

If you're a parent to a young child, then you know finding quiet times in the morning to read Scripture can be challenging. Perhaps set your alarm clock for

35

fifteen minutes prior to your child's typical wake-up time and use those few minutes to read the Bible. Or, if you have trouble waking early, you might seek out quiet, alone time before your day gets into full swing. Maybe this means reading a few verses on your smartphone in your car after you drop your kids off at school but before you walk into your office. Or maybe you do a trade-off with your spouse.

When our oldest daughter was very young, my wife and I would occasionally give each other a "time-out" so the other person could spend a few minutes in Scripture. It wasn't the time-out like we give children when they have disobeyed. Rather, one of us would feed our daughter breakfast and clean her up while the other went to the bedroom and read the Bible for a few minutes. In any case, reading the Bible for a few minutes each day sounds like a simple practice—and it is—but it can also be very difficult to implement if we're not intentional about planning it into our day.

Selfishness: A Marriage and Family Assassin

According to Merriam-Webster's dictionary, selfish can be defined as "concerned excessively or exclusively with oneself: seeking or concentrating on one's own advantage, pleasure, or well-being without regard for others." In Chapter 1 we discussed the idea that selfishness can very well be the root sin that leads us to work-life *im*balance (where *im*balance is the "fruit" of our selfishness).

Dennis and Barbara Rainey of FamilyLife have noted, "Selfishness is possibly the most dangerous threat to oneness in marriage."[1] That's a powerful statement! We are all born with a selfish nature. I have observed this over and over while watching my children play with their friends. I have also, unfortunately, observed this in my own life.

It's very easy for me to think to myself, "At least I don't do drugs," or, "At least I'm not cheating on my wife." However, I can be incredibly selfish, which can take a toll on my family life if I'm not careful. When I come home from work, I have a choice to make. I can A) plop down in the recliner and ignore my wife and children while watching TV the entire evening, or B) actively help my wife take care of our children and/or do things around the home that need doing.

This is where spiritual well-being comes into play. In Philippians we are instructed as Christians to "regard one another as more important than [ourselves]" and to not only "look out for [our] own personal interests, but also for the interests of others" (Philippians 2:3–4). This teaching is contrary to what our world seems to tell us. We are a "me-first" society. And, as noted earlier, we are born with a selfish nature that reinforces that we should put ourselves above others.

If we're being truthful with each other, then I must admit that coming home from a long day of work and simply chilling out in my recliner while watching TV sounds incredibly appealing on many days! However, I know my wife has been taking care of our children all day while I've been at work, and she likely needs a break from that. Additionally, I know my wife would like to talk with me and have me respond coherently instead of having me zoned out watching a mindless TV show. This two-way communication is a basic foundation of marriage.

Also, I know my daughters desire my attention, so we often color, play, and dance. It would be very selfish of me to ignore them each evening after work so that I can put my own interests first. And God would not be pleased if this were my routine after each work day. In fact, when Jesus was talking to his disciples, He said, "So you want first place? Then take the last place. Be the servant of all."* Wow! "*Be the servant of all.*" The best way for any husband or wife to play the role of servant is to start in his or her own home with their spouse and children.

One way I have found to combat selfishness is to pray for God to continually instill in me the fruit of His Spirit. Each morning I pray Galatians 5:22–23 for myself. In this prayer I am asking God that He would give me the ability to exhibit His love, joy, peace, patience, kindness, goodness, gentleness, faithfulness, and self-control in my life that day. Does that mean I'm a perfect prince every moment of every day? Not exactly. I can certainly get tired and grouchy like the rest of us. That said, increasing my spiritual well-being by praying this passage from Galatians over my day has certainly helped me to be more self*less* toward my

---

* Mark 9:35, *The Message*

family and coworkers. And when I'm being self*less*, it's much easier to balance my work and family.

Also, I don't let this morning prayer be my only time to pray. In 1 Thessalonians 5:17 we are told to "pray continually."[*] While a morning prayer is good, we are taught to pray consistently to God throughout our day. The typical day for most of us can be loud. By this I mean there's a lot of noise (coworkers, children, TV, radio, etc.) competing for our attention, and it's easy to drown out God if we're not careful. Yet by consistently praying to Him, we are more likely to remember our dependence upon God.

> *For each of us to establish a positive work-life balance, we must be aware of our spiritual well-being and be intentional about the choices that we make.*

For each of us to establish a positive work-life balance, we must be aware of our spiritual well-being and be intentional about the choices we make. This includes aligning our priorities with God's and decreasing our selfishness in favor of being self*less* to our family. So what does this look like? Here are a few possible action steps:

---

[*] NIV

Action Steps

- **Find a time for reading the Bible each day.**
  When could you realistically have a few minutes
  to yourself? Could your spouse help you make
  this happen by taking a few minutes to watch the
  kids while you go into another room? What kind
  of reading plan could you follow to accomplish
  this goal each day? Have you tried a Bible reading
  app on your phone, or maybe you could read one
  chapter from Proverbs or Psalms each day?

- **Continually pray for your family and your
  attitude (i.e., that you would be self*less*)
  throughout the day.** Do you start your day with
  prayer? Could you pray in the car on your way to
  work instead of listening to the radio? Or maybe
  you could listen to praise music or a sermon in
  the car to set your mind on the Lord at the start
  of your day. Could you pause during the day when
  you get frustrated or overwhelmed to ask God for
  help and patience? Would memorizing Galatians
  5:22–23 and praying it over yourself be helpful?

- **Spend time reading the Bible and praying as
  a family.** This would allow you to work on your
  spiritual well-being as a family. Consider reading a
  short passage of Scripture together each morning
  at the breakfast table or each night at the dinner
  table. Maybe take turns with your spouse putting
  your children to bed, then read a children's Bible
  story to them and pray with them.

- **Evaluate your priorities and plans.** Do they align with what God would want for your life? Do they honor His character and His Word? Is there anything you can do better to align your priorities with what God is calling you to do? Do you and your spouse need to spend some time in prayer about what your future looks like for your career and family?

Finally, a reminder: this chapter is the only non-negotiable in this book. You can be selective about which tips you want to implement from the chapters going forward. Maybe you'll put the upcoming chapter on exercise on the back burner and choose to focus on the emotional intelligence chapter instead. That's okay. However, aligning our priorities with His and decreasing our selfishness are crucial to the Christian's work-life balance, so make this chapter a priority.†

---

† If reading this chapter has left you asking questions about God, I would encourage you to check out the Invitation on page 107.

3

EXERCISE

I run because it's cheaper than therapy.
— Someone on the Internet

Drop and give me twenty push-ups! Okay, so that's probably not the first work-life balance strategy you wanted to read in this chapter. Don't worry; no push-ups are required—but they are optional! While many Americans struggle with work-life balance, we also struggle with fitting exercise into our schedules. According to a 2015 Centers for Disease Control and Prevention (CDC) poll about physical activity, half of all Americans (50.8%) do not get enough exercise.[1] This means half of those who read this book in the U.S. are not currently exercising on a regular basis.

A majority of us are aware of the health benefits of exercising. So why do we skip out on fitness? For some it is the fear of engaging in the act of exercise in front of others (e.g., in a crowded health club). For others it is the lack of know-how; that is, they do not know what type of exercise to do. And still for others it is a matter of motivation. However, for many of us the primary reason we do not exercise is related to one word: time. The desire is there, but our schedules are just too full.

You might be asking yourself the question, "If I am already stretched too thin at work and home, then why is this author asking me to add one *more* item to my already busy schedule?" This is certainly a valid question. After all, using exercise, an activity that has the potential to take an hour or more each time you do it, to help create better work-life balance sounds counterintuitive. So how does it work? The keys to exercise helping your work-life balance lie in reducing stress and increasing self-efficacy. I'll tell you more about those in a few minutes, but first let me tell you a story.

My Introduction to Regular Exercise

In one of my first jobs after graduating college, I worked for a gentleman named David Bass. David is a great guy, and he taught me a lot about how the "real world" works. But one of the greatest lessons he taught me was the importance of exercising on a regular basis.

Most days during lunch, David would go to the football stadium near our office and jog up and down the stadium steps multiple times. Now, that might not be your idea of a fun workout, but that's not the point I'm trying to make. Eager to learn and get face time with my boss, I joined David two to three times each week during his lunchtime exercise sessions at the football stadium. I have no idea how far we jogged or

44

how many steps we went up. But what I do know is that my productivity in the office always increased during those afternoons when I had taken part in the stadium-step madness earlier that day. Years later I asked David why he thought the stadium jogging made us so productive at work. He responded, "Jogging up and down the steps makes my problems get smaller."

I believe David is right. I was single when I worked for him, but I continued my exercise habit once I left that job and eventually moved into marriage and parenthood. As a single guy, I was thinking in terms of productivity at work, and exercise certainly helped with that. But now that I'm married with two small children, I couldn't help but think that exercise could help with work-life balance. So, naturally, with the help of some of my colleagues, I decided to research the effects of exercise on balancing work and life.

How Exercise Impacts Work-Life Balance

So what exactly did my boss, David, mean when he said exercise helps his problems get smaller? Was the stress-relief from exercise the key? Or did he feel more confident in handling what seemed like a big problem after he exercised? I believe the study I directed helps answer this.[2] One of the research findings of the study, while important, is not necessarily new information: exercise reduces our stress levels. That is certainly good to know, as stress often leads to work-life *im*balance. Stressors from our workplaces and homes are often to blame for our work-life *im*balance.

However, the other research finding from our study provides a major reason why exercise is so effective in helping us attain a better work-life balance: people who exercise on a regular basis have a greater sense of self-efficacy, which isn't to be confused with self-efficiency. As I mentioned in the *Harvard Business Review*, self-efficacy "refers to the sense that one is capable of taking things on and getting them done—and although self-efficacy is a matter of self-perception, it has real impact on reality."[3] Simply put, self-efficacy is the belief that you *can* make it through your workday, or that you *can* take care of your kids while your spouse is away. Many of the problems David faced in the workplace, several of which seemed rather large, began to look much smaller once his sense of confidence was amplified after an exercise session.

Exercise creates this sense of self-efficacy, or confidence, because we accomplish something each time we set out to exercise.[*] Remember the statistic from the beginning of the chapter? Half of all Americans do not exercise regularly. For many of us, the simple act of lacing up our shoes and getting out the door to exercise can create some level of empowerment. Then once we actually finish that Zumba class, jog those two miles, or complete that weight-lifting session, we feel as though we have really accomplished something. And the good news is

---

[*] Note: We have to actually follow through with the plan to exercise in order to get this sense of accomplishment.

that feeling of self-efficacy tends to carry over into other areas of our lives outside the specific exercise session we just completed. As David recounted, "an hour of exercise creates a feeling that lasts well beyond that hour spent [wherever you happen to exercise]." When faced with a tough obstacle at work or home, that sense of accomplishment may give you that extra bit of oomph that will help you overcome the challenge.

Here's an example: suppose you have a to-do list at work tomorrow that has ten items on it. Before going to bed tonight, you decide it would be beneficial for you to jog for twenty minutes throughout your neighborhood before you go into the office in the morning. Once you complete that jog, you get a sense of accomplishment. Not only did you jog somewhere between one and two miles, but you also remember that you could have slept a few extra minutes instead of going for that jog, but you chose to jog.

This sense of accomplishment carries over to your workplace when you get there and get ready to tackle that to-do list. You confront the to-do list with much greater confidence than if you had not earned that sense of self-efficacy earlier that morning. This might make the difference in you getting to leave work on time versus having to stay thirty to forty-five minutes late because you were less confident in your abilities.

And keep in mind that exercise does not have to be first thing in the morning as I mentioned in the example above. It can be during lunch, as David does, or after your workday is complete. Self-efficacy can be built at any point during the day and typically has a lasting effect. That said, know yourself: if you know that you find any excuse not to work out

> *Self-efficacy can be built at any point during the day and typically has a lasting effect.*

later in the day, then perhaps early in the morning is your best option. As my job and family have changed over time, so has my exercise routine. I now find that I must get up and exercise in the mornings if I want to fit exercise into my day. Otherwise, it will likely not happen.

A Biblical View

Research tells us that exercise is beneficial to our work-life balance, but how does our faith shape our view on exercise? In 1 Corinthians 9:25–27, Paul writes using the metaphor of an athlete training in order to teach us about spiritual self-discipline. Specifically, in verse 25 Paul mentions that "we do [our training] to get a crown that will last forever"[*] as opposed to a reward that will not last. What if we used this imagery to motivate us to use exercise as a way of obtaining a better work-life balance in regard to our spiritual lives?

---

[*] NIV

We could look at the reward that will not last, one result of exercise, as a good physical physique and strong cardiovascular system. Both of those results are great outcomes of exercise and contribute to our current quality of life. That said, the reality is that we will all one day get old and frail (my apologies for the downer!). However, what about the "crown that will last forever" as Paul mentions?

In the first chapter I mentioned that God wants us to focus on our relationship with our spouse and children (Genesis 2:24 and Deuteronomy 6:6–7). Perhaps the habit of exercise can mold you into the type of person who is less stressed at work and home and who can meet obstacles head-on because of self-efficacy, thus making you more available, both physically and emotionally, for your loved ones. An investment in your family is likely to fall under the umbrella of a "crown that will last forever." As such, perhaps the discipline of regular exercise can mold us into the type of spouse or parent who is able to invest quality time in those God has entrusted us with. Furthermore, it is likely this investment will reap benefits beyond your home. The increase in self-

> **Perhaps the discipline of regular exercise can mold us into the type of spouse or parent who is able to invest quality time in those God has entrusted us with.**

efficacy created by your exercise may serve to make you a better volunteer in your church and community.

The sentiment exists among some Christians that time spent exercising is time that could have been used for a better (i.e., holier, more worthy) purpose. And it is certainly true that any activity, including exercise, has the potential to take away time from other pursuits. On the other hand, some parents believe they must abandon their own pursuits in order to invest fully in their children. For instance, it's common for some parents to forego exercising so that they can completely devote themselves to raising their children. There's nothing truly wrong with that. I would much rather see a parent sacrifice exercise in order to raise their children instead of seeing a parent devote themselves to exercise to the neglect of spending time with their kids. That said, I encourage such sacrificial parents to work on finding time to exercise in the midst of their busy schedule. The act of spending a few minutes two to four days each week to take care of yourself can actually make you better able to take care of your children. A small change, such as a five-minute body-weight exercise routine first thing in the morning, might make the difference in a parent's level of confidence in balancing the demands of work and family.

And there certainly are areas of our lives more important than exercise. But I love how *The Message* paraphrases 1 Timothy 4:8: "Workouts in the gymnasium are useful, but a disciplined life in God is far more so, making you fit both today and forever." Spending time with God is without a doubt the priority, which is why the previous chapter in this book is non-negotiable. However, the verse above tells us there is undoubtedly value in exercise. We just have to find time to fit both time with God and time for exercise into our hectic schedules.

Let's Get Moving!

If you're already in the habit of exercising, then consider the previous 2,000 words as a good reminder of why your habit is a good one—and keep up the good work! Nonetheless, as a word of caution, don't let your exercise habit get to the point that it takes *too much* time away from your family and work.

If you've given up on exercising or have never been in the habit of exercising in the first place, then consider this a slight nudge toward slowly working your way into exercising. My advice is to simply get moving. You don't have to train to run a marathon or lift weights to bulk up like an NFL linebacker. The focus here is more on the psychological benefits of exercise as opposed to its physical and health aspects.

The first place to start is to know yourself. What I mean by this is to figure out what type of exercise you would enjoy and start from there. If you do not enjoy a particular form of exercise, then you likely will not reap its psychological benefits. I enjoy running two to four miles at a time because it gives me a chance to clear my head and pray. However, I know a lot of people detest even the thought of running. My wife is not a fan of long runs. She knows this and has structured her exercise time accordingly, choosing to take part in exercise classes such as Zumba and Pilates, or jogging on an elliptical machine at a gym while chatting with her friends.

Here are a few more action steps you can implement if you'd like to use exercise as a work-life balance strategy:

Action Steps

- **Ease in to your new exercise routine.** If you're new to exercise, or just getting back into the swing of things, take it easy. Trying to do too much too soon will likely cause you to form a negative impression about your new exercise habit. Overdoing it could lead you to become overly sore and will not create a positive feeling for you. Or, if you try to do too much and are unable to accomplish what you set out to do, you'll miss out on that feeling of self-efficacy. If you want to start jogging, don't go "all-in" and set out for a twelve mile run on your first day. Instead, try running for ten minutes and take a few walk breaks. Then you can build up time and/or distance from there. For new joggers, the "Couch to 5K" program is very popular. I am personally a fan of Jeff Galloway's run-walk method[4] and utilize it for most of my jogging.

- **Decide if you will exercise alone or in a group.** Think through whether you would enjoy exercising alone or with others. This might seem like a small detail, but it can make a difference as to whether you stick with your exercise habit or not. Some people benefit from the alone time that exercise can provide. If your job involves a lot of interaction with others throughout the day, you may enjoy forty-five minutes to yourself during your lunch break or shortly after work. On the other hand, group exercise classes provide individuals with a sense of camaraderie and are often seen as more fun. Decide what works best for you. As I previously mentioned, I appreciate the alone time offered by a short jog through my neighborhood, whereas my wife enjoys the added social benefit and accountability offered by using the elliptical at the gym while chatting with one or more of her friends.

- **Figure out what will provide accountability.** Some of us need more accountability to exercise than others. There was a time in my life where I would consistently go for long runs by myself without anyone having to hold me accountable for showing up for the run. At another stage, I needed accountability, and I knew that full well. During that stage of life, I joined an exercise facility that was strictly class-based and cost me a significant fee each month. This accomplished two goals: a) my wallet was tied into the exercise so I was more likely to go (i.e., I didn't want to waste my money!), and b) being in a class setting kept me from slacking off or loafing through the workout. For some, a fitness tracker or a visual calendar may help you stick to your exercise plans.

- **Pursue cost-effective methods.** I just noted how I've been a member of a gym that had a significant monthly fee. However, that doesn't mean you have to do the same. I am now a member at a gym that costs me one-third as much as that pricey gym. Many cost-effective ways of exercising are available for those who want to invest time but not money into their exercise habit. Running, jogging, or walking are about the cheapest forms of exercise in existence. Lace up your shoes, put one foot in front of the other, and go! A word of practical advice: make sure you have good running shoes.* Wearing old or ill-fitting shoes will lead to injuries that will cause you to not want to exercise. Bodyweight exercises are even cheaper than jogging. Air squats, push-ups, and crunches in your garage or living room are free and provide a great workout. Many websites, blogs, and apps offer suggestions for workouts, so you don't even have to think much about it.

- **Determine the time you will devote to exercise.** You do *not* have to spend an hour per day working out to reap the psychological benefits of reduced stressed and increased self-efficacy. A twenty-minute jog two to three times per week might be good for some. Others might enjoy doing thirty minutes of bodyweight exercises at home. For those who are really time-strapped, try

---

* A $125 pair of good running shoes will give you four hundred to six hundred miles of exercise. If you jog two-and-a-half miles three times per week for a year, then you will be at 390 miles per year. That means your $125 investment will last you at least one year! That's only $2.40 per week!

the popular "7-Minute Workout"[5] that can be done with common household and office furniture. Remember, the goal here (at least for this book) is not to become the next great athlete because of your training. Rather, we're looking for increased self-efficacy and decreased stress levels, which can usually be achieved with short spurts of exercise.

Finally, be sure to consult your healthcare provider prior to beginning a new exercise routine. The main encouragement here is just to get moving! You might even make it a family affair and take a family walk after dinner to get some exercise and spend time with your spouse and kids. Ultimately, understanding the value that exercise brings to your work-life balance may be your best motivator.

4

EMOTIONAL INTELLIGENCE

*And when it comes to success in personal life,
I would bet emotional intelligence
matters more than IQ.*

— Daniel Goleman,
New York Times bestselling author

Suppose you ask a family member to take care of a household chore while you're away for the day. When you arrive home, you notice the chore has *not* been done. Once you get inside, you see your family member sitting on the couch with their head in their hands. Do you:

A) Question them about why they didn't handle the chore you asked them to do?

B) Take care of the chore yourself out of disappointment?

C) Try your best *not* to engage with them since you noticed their downcast demeanor?

D) Attempt to engage in conversation and find out what's wrong?

This seems like an easy answer, doesn't it? Of course, if we're answering this question in a group setting, we'd likely all answer, "D." We'd try to find out why our loved one appeared to be down. The reality for many of us, myself included, is that many times our response to a situation like this sounds like options A, B, or C. That is, many of us would be angry or frustrated at the person for not doing as we had asked. And this response would likely remain the same if we changed the context of that scenario from a household chore to a workplace duty or church volunteer activity.

In our fast-paced world we often take the self-centered approach and think, "Why didn't they just do what I asked?" instead of attempting to figure out why the person appears downcast. For many of us—again, this includes me—we're so concerned with getting something done that we fail to take into account that the person in the scenario may be dealing with a few negative emotions. This is why I want to talk about the concept of emotional intelligence (EI).

What is Emotional Intelligence?

Emotional intelligence in its most basic form can be understood as "the ability to manage the impact of emotions on our relationships with others."[1] Or, as my colleague Hank Clemons puts it, "EI is being smart about our emotions and the emotions of others." This includes how we express ourselves, handle social relationships, deal with challenges, and use emotional information.

Although the topic of EI has gained a lot of traction in the popular press, its roots are in academic psychology. And while EI is heavily researched by psychologists, it fits neatly within our Christian faith. In fact, one pastor has noted that he believes "the whole emotional intelligence language . . . is actually the fruit of the Spirit played out in psychological terms."[2] Other Christians often refer to biblical intelligence, or biblical wisdom, as synonymous with EI.

Several dimensions make up the umbrella term of EI. And depending on which book or article you read on the topic, those facets may be named differently to reflect the proprietary nature of the EI material you're reading. However, almost every model of EI contains three core dimensions and can help us pursue work-life balance: self-awareness, self-management, and social awareness.

Self-Awareness

Being aware of our emotions is a great place to start. After all, as Plato said, "Know thyself." Furthermore, John Calvin emphasized the importance of knowing ourselves, remarking that our knowledge of God and knowledge of ourselves make up the entirety of wisdom.[3] So what exactly is self-awareness in the context of EI? Self-awareness is our capacity not only to recognize our emotions (i.e., thoughts and feelings), but also to recognize how our emotions impact those around us. This entails knowing our strengths and limitations. What roles do you regularly play that you would categorize as strengths? How about weaknesses? What type of emotional responses do these various roles prompt?

When our oldest daughter was a toddler, I was very active in helping to take care of her (and I still am today). Changing her diapers and getting her down for naptime were the norm, and I was fairly good at those roles. On the other hand, bath time was not my favorite. I cannot put my finger on it, but if I were the one who had to bathe her, I would end up becoming very frustrated by the end of bath time because, for whatever reason, bathing her was not one of my strengths. Maybe it was because I wasn't good at getting the baby shampoo out of her hair or that I was unable to control her wiggly and slippery little body. This frustration that was a result of bath time would carry over into the rest of our evening and impact my interactions with my family. I talked with my wife and expressed my feelings about bath time, and we agreed that I would be in charge of other tasks instead of bathing our daughter on a routine basis. However, this didn't mean I got a free pass never to be in charge of bath time.

Some of you may be thinking, "Why didn't he just suck it up and give his daughter a bath?" The reality is that at that stage of our daughter's life, I was much better at handling certain childcare responsibilities (e.g., changing diapers) than I was others (e.g., bath time). There were certainly times when I did have to "suck it up" and be the one to bathe our daughter. If my wife didn't feel well, I didn't invoke the "no bath time clause" and make her bathe our daughter anyway. In cases like that, I'd "suck it up" and be in charge of bath time. The point I'm trying to make is that I finally became aware that giving my daughter a bath would usually lead me to become less than effective emotionally throughout that evening. It's not that I was lazy or selfish. Rather, I knew that this particular childcare activity was one that had the potential to cause negative emotions within me.

Being self-aware and knowing what enhances and what brings down your mood is an excellent way to build your EI. However, it is not a license for us to automatically remove everything from our lives that frustrates us. For example, early on bath time was not something that elevated my mood, so I worked with my wife to find other childcare activities that I was better at so that I could still be a supportive spouse. That said, it would be impossible to tell my wife that *all* _____ responsibilities frustrate me and I should not have to do them.* This would make me a very unsupportive spouse.† However, I believe it is acceptable and wise to be strategic about evaluating what roles throw your emotions into a nosedive and then work to adjust those roles.

We cannot eliminate all of the roles that cause frustration, but we can be strategic in identifying events that lead to frustration and, from time-to-time, adjusting our level of involvement in those events. This could lead to a somewhat small change, such as being in charge of feeding your toddler instead of bathing him or her. Or, this self-awareness may lead

---

* Fill in the blank for your situation: childcare, landscaping, grocery shopping, handyman, washing clothes, etc.
† Not to mention a huge jerk!

to a large change, such as changing jobs to avoid a role that conflicts with your personality or to avoid a long, emotionally draining commute. In other words, learn to know what brings your mood down. That sounds simple, but people often can take a passive stance on figuring out why their emotions, whether positive or negative, are the way they are.

Self-Management

Being aware of our emotions provides a nice transition to the EI dimension of self-management. As I previously noted, being aware of what affects our emotional state can lead to changes in our various roles. However, we will not always have the ability to immediately change our situation. You may not be able to eliminate your hour-long work commute because doing so would leave you without a job. This is where self-management comes into play. The self-management dimension of EI helps us focus on managing our emotions pertaining to those aspects of life that cannot (or will not) change. We can use the dimension of self-management to direct our behavior in a positive manner and to be flexible when we are in less than desirable situations.

In a different season of my life, I had a scenario in which I could not negotiate for a change in responsibilities. Shortly before my wife and I got married, I took a new job in a different city from where we would be living. The job came with both an increase in pay and an upgraded title. However, the job also came with an hour-long commute each way. This meant I woke up earlier than before and got home later than I would have liked. While I enjoyed the job, I quickly began to resent the commute. Unfortunately, I was not in a position to make a switch to a job closer to our home.

As such, I began to reframe how I looked at my situation. If I were not managing my emotions (i.e., self-management), then it would have been very easy for me to become dissatisfied and agitated, both at work and at home. Instead, I tried to look for the silver lining.[‡] I began to think through how fortunate I was to have a steady job and income. So each time the negative thoughts crept into my mind, or I got down about the upcoming one-hour commute to or from work, I intentionally reframed the thought. I shifted my focus to the fact that I had a job on the other end of that commute to work and that I had a house and loving wife on the commute back home.

I tried to take this same self-management approach with both of my daughters and the late nights we had with each of them during their first few months of life. Any of you who are parents can likely recall those first few months of your child's life, when he or she would sleep all day but decide to stay awake all night. That's a pretty tough season for most us, and I would be lying if I told you I never got stressed or irritable during that time.[§] There were nights when I did not handle the crying and screaming as well as I would have liked. But I did find it helpful to reframe the situation in a positive light by reminding myself of the gift of children God gave us (Psalms 127:3).

[‡] Cliché, I know! But it works to take this approach!
[§] Ask my wife . . . she will tell you!

If you've been in, or can imagine yourself in, the situations I've described above, then you can see where the possibility exists for disruptive behavior to occur because of your mood state. Disruptive behavior could take the form of yelling at your spouse and/or children or passive-aggressive behavior toward your family. In any case, the end result of self-management is to curb this disruptive behavior.

I believe God speaks to this in Proverbs 10:19. In this verse we are taught that "the prudent hold their tongues."** What's so special about holding our tongues, and how does this relate to self-management? When I googled "prudent," the first result defined it as "acting with or showing *care and thought for the future*" (emphasis added). Care and thought for the future! If I cannot regulate my emotion enough so that I can see the positive in having a child for whom I am privileged to care for, sometimes staying up at night to walk and bounce to pacify her, then this can create a domino effect that can impact my future with my wife and daughters. If left unchecked, negative emotions created by these types of situations can lead to resentment and anger that causes verbal outbursts which can disrupt our family's future. Therefore, I must be prudent and manage my emotions for the good of those around me and for the future of our relationships.

** NIV

Social Awareness and Empathy

The two dimensions of EI previously discussed deal with the awareness and management of our emotions. But what about your spouse's emotions? Your child's emotions? Your colleague's emotions? This is where social awareness comes into play. As you may be able to guess, social awareness is our ability to identify the emotions other people are experiencing. One of the biggest adjustments we can make to increase our awareness of others' emotions is to work on increasing our empathy. While social awareness helps us recognize what others are going through, empathy takes this a step further and helps us to understand the perspective of others and what they are going through. That is, not only can we name the emotion (for example, sadness), but we are able to feel, to some degree, that person's emotion.

> *I must be prudent and manage my emotions for the good of those around me and for the future of our relationships.*

In the opening paragraph of this chapter, I gave an example in which your loved one was sitting on the couch with their head in their hands. A majority of those reading this book could pick out the emotion your loved one is feeling and put a fairly accurate title to it, which is a good start. But simply identifying that they are sad, angry, etc. is not always enough to help us regulate *our* emotional response. Empathizing with them—putting ourselves in their shoes—is the next step and is the antidote that helps us prevent a destructive emotional reaction on our part.

If I arrive home and notice my wife sitting on the couch with her head in her hands, then I know she's sad. But, if I stop there with only identifying her as being sad, then that makes it easier for me to walk into another room and not engage her in conversation. This behavior on my part would be similar to the "ignore it and it will go away" approach to dealing with life. It's not until I can understand and possibly even feel her sadness that I will be able to respond appropriately. If I consider what might have made her sad—maybe she received some bad news or had a rough day with the kids—and think about how I'd feel, then I might realize that she probably wants a hug or the chance to talk about what's upsetting her.* By being socially aware and empathizing with her emotions, I can handle my emotions more appropriately instead of just being angry that the chore did not get finished.

Support for Emotional Intelligence

The idea of social awareness and empathy may sound a bit touchy-feely to you, and perhaps touchy-feely isn't your style. Nonetheless, empathy is a concept with biblical support (see Proverbs 14:31 and 17:17). God speaks in the Bible about caring for

---

* Or maybe she just wants to go walk around Target for an hour by herself.

others and treating others well. We see this in Colossians 3:12 when we're instructed to clothe ourselves with compassion, kindness, humility, gentleness, and patience. These attributes are tough to display without having some measure of empathy in our lives. For example, if I cannot empathize with my loved one from the opening example, then why would I be willing to extend gentleness and patience to them for not completing the chore?

Not only does EI have biblical support, but it also has support from the social sciences. My own data,[4] along with studies from other researchers,[5,6] shows that a person's level of EI is a great predictor of work-life balance. In particular, social awareness has a particularly strong impact on work-life balance because it aids in reducing the friction between our loved ones or coworkers and us. In addition, those people in my study who had high levels of self-awareness and self-management were less stressed than those who did not have a high EI.

> *Social awareness has a particularly strong impact on work-life balance because it aids in reducing the friction between our loved ones or coworkers and us.*

But enough talk about research support. How can you increase your EI in an effort to help balance work and life?

Action Steps

- **Identify your strengths and weaknesses.** What roles give you energy and what roles lead to increased frustration? What roles should you reduce your involvement in through negotiation at home and work? Remember, we can't wipe *all* frustrating activities off our plates. So which one or two roles should you target? Ask God for wisdom in this area (see James 1:5).

- **Expand your circle of empathy.** I love Jessica Stillman's idea of expanding our circle of empathy.[7] There are various areas in which it is easy for us to empathize. If you were bullied in school, then you're probably able to empathize with a teenager going through the same situation. But there are other areas and issues where we are less empathetic. Stillman's idea is to try to see the perspective of those with whom you have less natural empathy. For example, you might try to look with empathy at the violence in sub-Saharan Africa. This does not mean that you're looking to take the side of those committing the violence or to validate their behavior. Rather, it's a brain-stretching exercise that forces you to look at situations involving people with whom you may have little in common.

- **Reframe negative situations.** This can sound a bit hokey, but give it a try. If you make fifty thousand dollars per year and get angry that you're not making sixty-five thousand, remember that at least you have a job and that you earn more than a majority of individuals in America. Be grateful for that fifty thousand! Will this thought process magically put more money in your pockets? No! But it will help you have a more positive frame of mind and a better emotional state.

- **Increase your emotional literacy.** Describe a frustrating situation accurately using only three words. For example, if my wife and I go shopping, and we go to seven different stores looking for that perfect pair of shoes for her, then I may be tempted to have an emotional outburst and exclaim, "This shoe hunt is soooo stupid!" Is her hunt for the right pair of shoes stupid? Not really. What if I thought, "I feel impatient," instead? That accurately gets to the root of the issue. Using those three words, I am now accepting responsibility for how I feel. Realizing that I'm the impatient one allows me the opportunity to deal with my impatience. If I find myself in this scenario, perhaps it's time to ask God for an extra dose of patience to help me get through the shopping trip.[*]

---

[*] Just like in Chapter 2, I'll pray Galatians 5:22–23 over myself.

5

TIME MANAGEMENT

There is no blueprint for all Christians in the use of their time. . . . So each of us should consider the basic components of a productive Christian life and prayerfully set specific goals.
— Charles Hummel in *Tyranny of the Urgent*

Time is one of the most common issues cited as contributing to a lack of work-life balance. Within each twenty-four-hour day, we find ourselves in a real-life, five-thousand-piece jigsaw puzzle trying to fit the pieces together the right way so that we can eat, take care of our children, call those clients, take care of others (e.g., aging parents), find time with our spouse, sleep, find time with God, finish that project, take care of ourselves, submit that expense report, pick up the dry-cleaning, attend that meeting at church, etc. That's a lot to fit into one day! It seems that a never-ending cycle of people and events need or want our attention.

The good news is that I've figured out a way to extend each twenty-four-hour day by an extra five hours! Okay, so that's not really the case. However, I do want to share with you a few strategies I have used in my life to manage my time better. I still only have twenty-four hours each day; I have just learned to use those hours more effectively. I am certainly not saying that I completely have this time-management thing all figured out. In fact, at one point in my adult life I would have laughed hysterically at the idea of me writing anything on time management. And other authors and books certainly go into much more detail on this topic than this book has space for. Nonetheless, I want to share some simple and practical approaches to better managing your time. But first, let's look at how we view time.

A Different View on Time

No one can debate the fact that each day contains twenty-four hours, and that is how we traditionally structure our schedules. Furthermore, that is typically where we get our "shortage of time" dilemma from (i.e., "There's not enough time in the *day*."). So let's think about time in a broader perspective for just a moment. In Psalms 39:5 we see that our life is "a mere breath" of time. In other words, we're only going to be alive for a short period. I know that sounds like a downer, but let it shift your perspective on your day-to-day activities at your workplace.

As Charles Hummel so eloquently put it in *Tyranny of the Urgent*, "Our dilemma [about time management] goes deeper than shortage of time; it is basically a problem of *priorities*" (emphasis added). I continuously have daily and weekly priorities. These priorities may be to grade a stack of case studies, unload the dishwasher, get a report reviewed by the deadline, etc. Those priorities are fine, and they allow me to be effective at work and home. But they are short-term priorities. What are my long-term priorities, and what should they look like?

In the United States our short-term and long-term priorities often revolve around the workplace: complete the XYZ Project by next Tuesday, get a promotion, sell the most widgets this fiscal year, make partner at the firm. None of these priorities are inherently wrong. Working hard is *not* a sin. In fact, those priorities I just listed will all likely lead to some level of financial reward that helps you provide for

> **God has instructed us to make family a priority.**

your family. And as we discovered in Chapter 1, providing for our family is important to God (see 1 Timothy 5:8). But are these priorities being met at the expense of our family? Just because we have enough money to buy necessities for our family, are we available to spend time with them, too? As we also saw in Chapter 1, God has instructed us to make family a priority.

I believe God would have us give top billing to the long-term priority of family.* I've said before and have even posted on social media that one of my life's priorities is that my daughters always know they are

---

* Recall from Chapter 1: Genesis 2:24 and Deuteronomy 6:6–7

more important to me than my work. That is a long-term priority that shapes my short-term (or daily) priorities. I know without a doubt that this is a God-pleasing priority and one that is of the utmost importance. However, Hummel's wise words come back to haunt me from time-to-time: "Your greatest danger is letting the urgent things crowd out the important."

Those "urgent things" can get in the way of our priorities, whether a family or work priority. For example, if I'm consistently bringing papers home to grade each evening to the neglect of my wife and daughters, then I'm letting the urgent tasks of work get in the way of my priority of family. It may be that I feel the

> *Those "urgent things" can get in the way of our priorities, whether a family or work priority.*

need to bring papers home to grade because there's not enough time in the day to get them graded at my office on campus. Perhaps there's not "enough time in the day" at work because I'm not using my time efficiently.

Or maybe you're a stay-at-home parent who always feels like there's more to do than there is time in the day. Maybe your three kids have soccer on Monday, ballet on Tuesday, church on Wednesday, and piano on Thursday. And most Saturdays involve a birthday party, soccer game, or recital. Are there activities that can be cut out or done less frequently to create more family time?

So how can we structure a typical day to free up more time at home and/or reduce the urge to bring work home? Here are a few strategies that have been helpful for me both in my working life as an academic and my prior working life in sales.

Action Steps

- **Pray for discernment about your time.** I'm willing to bet that you were not expecting prayer to be the first action step on time management. In *Tyranny of the Urgent*, Hummel quotes P.T. Forsyth as having said, "The worst sin is prayerlessness." This is due to our prayerlessness being a sign of self-sufficiency and not needing God's help. However, if God can help us in other areas of our lives, then why shouldn't we call on Him for help with managing our time? Charles Stanley has noted that the scheduling of our time is something we should ask for God's wisdom on.[1] While the Bible will not tell us explicitly when to schedule a staff meeting or when to set aside time to work on a project, asking for God's guidance (through prayer) on how to use your time efficiently will make us sensitive to His leading. This prayerfulness will likely help shift our priorities over time so that they align with His.

- **Stop multitasking.** I am guilty of violating this and have to remind myself to stop multitasking on a regular basis. On the surface, multitasking makes sense. I mean, who wouldn't want to do three tasks at once and get done with them all (presumptively sooner than doing each task separately). But did you know that when we multitask it takes us on average 25 percent *longer* to finish each task than if we would have done each task separately?[2] A psychological experiment actually puts that number higher, stating that multitasking makes us up to 40 percent *slower*.[3] Ouch! Instead, make a list of each day's or week's tasks and order them with the greatest priority. Then, do each task one at a time! Sounds simple, doesn't it? It's actually pretty difficult to do and takes some practice. For most of us our natural inclination will be to multitask. Assigning a specific amount of time to each task is also helpful. It may also be helpful for many of the tasks to be done without interruptions (see the next action step.)

- **Manage interruptions and distractions.** Even when you take the step of making a list and doing one task at a time, you still have to deal with unwanted interruptions and distractions. A study conducted by research and consulting firm Basex showed that interruptions cost U.S. workplaces $588 billion per year.[*] That's a lot of money lost at the hand of interruptions. However, think about the cost in terms of lost minutes and hours for you personally. How often are you interrupted during an average workday? And does this keep you from leaving your job on time? If you're

---

[*] Yes, that's billion with a "b"!

losing thirty to forty-five minutes each day due to interruptions and also are unable to leave work on time, then there's a numerical cost of interruptions to you and an incentive to do something about it. Of course, interruptions of some type will happen, and it is impossible to completely eliminate them. Try reducing the number of interruptions and distractions with these tips:

o Turn email off for forty-five-minute blocks of time, thus limiting incoming distractions.

o Set up "time-lock worktime." Time-management author Edward Brown advocates this idea of locking in a set time where the door is closed and you allow no interruptions other than true emergencies. If your workplace is an "open door" workplace or if you work in a cubicle, then this takes a little more planning. Find a conference room where you can close the door, or work from a local coffee shop (assuming you have the flexibility to work off-site and don't get distracted in coffee shops).

o Just say no! This can make us feel uncomfortable at first. I used to say yes to literally everything a coworker would ask. "Hey, Russell, do you want to go get coffee in the break room?" "Hey, Russell, do you want to work on this research paper with me?" But once I learned how to say no, and that it was okay to say no, managing my time became much easier. It's okay to be strategically selfish with your time. A faith-based book imploring you to be selfish seems a bit counterintuitive. I'm not giving you a free pass to ignore every request for your time. We certainly all have responsibilities to our supervisor, spouse, and so on. But I encourage you to figure out where and when you can strategically say no. You'll find more time to spend on those items you deem most important.

- **Outsource.** Are there tasks at work (or home) that you're reluctant to give up control over? Now may be a good time to see which tasks you can delegate or outsource. I used to be unwilling to let anyone do any of my work for me. This means I would often spend approximately an hour each week at the copy machine. Then I decided to delegate my copying to our graduate assistants. Voila! I just found an extra hour each week. My buddy Don Moors took a similar approach at his home. He travels during the week for work and found that yardwork was taking up several hours of the time he was home and could spend with his wife and son. Therefore, he outsourced his yardwork to a landscaping company and now has an extra two to three hours per week to devote to his home life. You might choose to use Saturday mornings as a time to outsource some of the household chores to your other family members. For example, our four-year-old is in charge of putting away her clean dishes, her clean laundry, and straightening up the toys in the living room and her room. That saves my wife and I at least thirty minutes of household work each day. What tasks can you outsource at work or home?

- **Plan family time.** Make it a priority and put it on the schedule. Maybe you start the tradition of Friday family movie nights, Saturday morning pancake breakfasts, or Taco Tuesdays for dinner. What if you also plan annual family time such as a visit to the zoo every April? Identify how you can include more family time and then put it in writing on your calendar.

Your unique situation will require you to tweak some of the strategies. Each of these tips may not be feasible for you. For example, if you're a receptionist then it will likely be difficult for you to set up a time-lock and disappear for a couple of hours. Or perhaps your family budget is extremely tight and you don't feel that you can pay to outsource your yardwork. Evaluate the strategies above and see which ones may work for your particular situation.

6

CAREER MANAGEMENT

*The problem with winning the rat race is . . .
you're still a rat.*

— Lily Tomlin

Of all the tips and strategies in this book, this chapter presents the one that is least likely to be accepted and most likely to be dismissed. Plain and simple, in this chapter I'm going to ask you to consider making career changes. Some are minimal; others arc more drastic. While most of us want to attain a better work-life balance, many are unwilling to give up our current way of life, which is supported

> **While most of us want to attain a better work-life balance, many of us are unwilling to give up our current way of life.**

in many cases by our long working hours. That said, read this chapter and see if a career alteration, or even just a small shift, might work to help you have a better work-life balance.

As discussed, work-life *im*balance is often a result of working too many hours. After all, if we're physically or mentally at work, then that is time we're not physically or mentally present with our spouse or children. And, while I offered a few thoughts in the previous chapter on how to better manage our time, the reality is that some situations call for more radical measures.

Turning off email for an hour once per day to reduce interruptions might give you back four to five hours of time each week, and that's great if you're working forty-hour workweeks. However, if your average workweek is eighty hours, then that four to five hours gained is perhaps less impactful (i.e., you're still working seventy-five hours per week!). My guess is that those who work sixty to seventy-five hours a week are either:

1) workaholics who are okay with those long hours, or

2) reluctantly working that many hours to support their lifestyle but not necessarily enjoying the fact that they have to work so many hours.

If you're in Group A, then my advice is to examine your heart to figure out why you feel compelled to work so many hours. Additionally, seek advice from a Christian counselor. You may suffer from an overbearing desire to achieve or perform with pride at its root. If left unchecked, such pride could destroy your family, and not to mention your health. Perhaps spending time with God and working on your spiritual well-being (the focus of Chapter 2) and/or talking with a pastor or Christian counselor may be beneficial to you. In order for a downshift to be effective for a workaholic, some soul-searching and heart change must first take place.

> *Downshifting in the context of a career involves an intentional shift in some aspect of a person's working life in order to have more time with their family and/or to reduce one's stress levels.*

If you're in Group B and are working too many hours to support a lifestyle, then downshifting your career might be the ticket for you. But be forewarned: downshifting can come at a cost.

What Is a Downshift?

Downshifting in the context of a career involves an intentional shift in some aspect of a person's working life in order to have more time with their family and/or to reduce one's stress levels. This looks differently in various downshifting scenarios.

For example, my friend Mark Yenny was the owner of a small business that installed high-end, custom designer wallcoverings. This small business was financially rewarding for Mark but cost him a lot in terms of time with his family, in addition to sleepless nights as a result of business-related stress. Mark downshifted by giving up his small business in favor of working for someone else. Among other benefits, this gave him back weekends with his family and the ability to get a good night's sleep.

Another friend, Philip Craft, is a physical education teacher and former football coach. While Philip absolutely loves football, he told me he gave up coaching because it kept him from seeing his child as much as he would like. In his words, "It broke my heart every night that I would come home from practice and my daughter would already be asleep in bed." Giving up his coaching position meant giving up a hobby he enjoys, as well as a financial stipend associated with the position. Nonetheless, he says those benefits pale in comparison to the newfound time he has to spend with his daughter.

As a result of both Mark and Philip's downshifts, they were able to spend more time with their families while also reducing their levels of work responsibility. These benefits are the positive aspects of downshifting. However, it's important to realize that downshifting often comes with a reduction in income, which is often followed by a need to reduce household spending to some degree. These are the perceived negative aspects of downshifting. Therefore, I advise those who are thinking about downshifting to consider their options prayerfully and have an in-depth discussion with their spouse about its pros and cons. In other words, do not rush into downshifting because it typically results in some level of financial repercussions.

Types of Downshifting

Authors Amy Saltzman[1] and Scott Behson[2] have both written about downshifting in detail and provide us with a nice glimpse of what downshifting can look like for various people. For example, some people downshift by back-tracking, a form of self-demotion where the person intentionally takes a step down on the career ladder. This was made famous in the summer of 2014 when tech company executive Max Schireson stepped down as CEO of MongoDB and took a lower position, both in terms of title and pay, within the company. In an industry where CEOs are expected to put on a strong face and work long hours, Schireson noted, "Life is about choices. Right now, I choose to spend more time with my family and am confident that I can continue to have a meaningful and rewarding work life while doing so."[3]

And this doesn't just apply to executives. Amanda Varnadore, an elementary school teacher, made the decision to give up a full-time position for a half-time teaching position in order to spend more time with her son. Both Max and Amanda had good jobs they enjoyed, and both gave up those jobs for lesser jobs in the name of spending more time with family. That's the back-tracker of downshifting.

Another form of downshifting is the practice of plateauing. In the case of someone plateauing, no real demotion happens. The downshifting practice of plateauing does not involve having to take a lower job than the one you currently have. Instead, the plateauer simply foregoes a promotion or takes a lateral move to a job that likely will prohibit them from future promotions. The cost to the plateauer is future promotions and raises. However, the benefit is increased time away from work.

This was the case with Larry Powell. Larry worked for one of the largest banks in the United States and was in a position that required him to regularly put in sixty-hour workweeks, causing a strain on his family life. In Larry's case, he took another job within the bank with better hours that was considered a lateral move, but one that would all but eliminate him from consideration for future promotions within that bank. In the words of one of his supervisors, it would be "career suicide." Now with better working hours, Larry is happy with the move and is fine with plateauing within his company.

Finally, downshifting can include the career-shifter. These downshifters make small changes to their careers instead of the drastic changes of back-trackers. Nevertheless, these small changes tend to pay big dividends in terms of the time they get to spend with their family. The earlier example of Philip is a great illustration of career-shifting. Philip was a P.E. teacher and football coach. When he gave up the coaching position, he still had the P.E. teacher position. This wasn't a demotion, and he didn't cut his working status from full-time to half-time. He just gave up one facet of his job that was taking up a lot of his time. Again, this change certainly came with an economic cost when he gave up coaching and the associated stipend, but the gain was increased family time.

If you think downshifting is a work-life balance strategy for you, take these thoughts into consideration:

Action Steps

- **Pray.** Spend time with God and ask for wisdom to discern whether downshifting is the right move for you.[*] It's possible that God wants you to stay in your current job for a bit longer before downshifting. Or perhaps He will lead you to downshift immediately. Pray and ask Him for the right timing (see Proverbs 21:5.)

- **Talk with your spouse.** I'm going to go out on a limb here and say that making a career move without first talking with your spouse is not going to go as smoothly as you'd like. It's important to include your spouse in a decision such as downshifting. Pray with your spouse, and pray separately from your spouse. Make a pros-and-cons list of what could happen as a result of your downshift. Yes, downshifting will provide you with more time outside work, but it may decrease your household income too. A pros-and-cons list will help you know what to expect.

---

[*] Remember James 1:5

- **Manage your expectations.** To the point above, remember that there will likely be financial ramifications for you and your family as a result of you or your spouse downshifting. Know this and prepare accordingly. For example, early in our marriage my wife was a high school teacher and the sponsor of the cheerleading squad. While she enjoyed leading the squad, it was a huge time commitment for her. When she decided to shift away from leading the cheerleading squad, we knew it would free up her afternoons and evenings, but we also knew she would no longer get the five-thousand-dollar stipend that came with the position she was giving up. We were completely okay with that and figured that into our budget. To both of us, her time was more important than the money.

- **Stay employed.** Downshifting is *not* the act of quitting your job, becoming unemployed, and living off the land. Downshifters are still employed to some degree, and many downshifters are employed by the same company they worked for prior to downshifting. That's not to say that God might lead you to leave employment all together—that's possible. But in the context of downshifting you're still employed whether part-time or full-time. The goal is to shift the way you spend your work-related time in order to free up time for family and possibly even ministry opportunities.

- **Don't slack off at work.** Downshifters do *not* use "family first" as a reason to perform shoddy work for their employers, as that would not be honoring to God. In Ecclesiastes 9:10, God instructs us to work with all our might. While I limit the number of hours I work each week, I make sure my employer gets a solid work effort from me. This shows up in my positive teaching evaluations and research publications each semester. My colleagues know that I'm a Christian and have a family-first mentality. So if I were to slack off at work, how would that shape their view of Christianity? I never want to do anything that would give me the reputation of being a hypocrite or lazy; however, I'm proud of the reputation that I both value my family and am also committed to my job.

- **Adjust your definition of success.** Our Western society tends to define success in terms of wealth and titles. Think about it: when we meet someone new, we typically ask, "What do you do?" so that we can ascertain their career status. Personally, I have to constantly fight the urge to define my own success in terms of where I work and how much money I make. However, I always come back around to my personal view of success: having my wife and daughters know I value them above my work.

Maybe downshifting is right for you or your spouse. Perhaps it isn't. This is not a call for everyone to downshift. And remember, there's nothing fundamentally wrong or sinful about climbing the career ladder. Many godly men and women are at the top of their companies and industries. The goal is to find a healthy balance between work and non-work time and commitments.

7

REST AND FINANCES

With this chapter I want to give you two items to think about that can help you find a better balance between work and life. I will tell you up front that I do not have the answer to the *when* and *how* of these thoughts. That is, we all have various schedules, are in different life stages, and live in different places, so it's hard to give you a prescription that says, "Do X, Y, and Z." But I can give you the *why* behind these two thoughts on work-life balance. Then you can decide how to make adjustments in your life to achieve better work-life balance.

I'll discuss rest, first, offering some tips for how to slow down as well as literally get more sleep.

Then I'll touch on finances and provide some resources for trying to reduce some of the stress that can come from working more hours to earn enough money and budgeting what you spend.

Rest

> *Everyone has experienced seasons of life when rest is earnestly needed but not found . . .*
> *If such seasons have become the norm for you, perhaps you ought to reconsider the values that inform your decisions in life.*
> — John Scott Redd, President of Reformed Theological Seminary, Washington, D.C. campus[*]

> *Remember to take care of yourself.*
> *You can't pour from an empty cup.*
> — TobyMac, Grammy Award-Winning Artist

If you can't tell from the preceding quotes, I'm encouraging you to rest. What was that noise I just heard? Oh, that was you laughing out loud at me. In a world in which we're always connected and have schedules filled up by our employers and family, finding rest is difficult (and I'm preaching to the choir with this part of the book!). I love sleeping late and taking naps, but with two daughters under the age of five, that's just not happening very often. We can find multiple verses in the Bible about rest—see Psalms 62:5, 116:7, and Mark 6:31—yet many of us find it so hard to do. Perhaps it is our schedules, our work-first mentality, or something else.

Again, I don't know what this looks like for you because I don't know your exact situation, but let me encourage you to rest. For me, this means going to bed just a little earlier. My wife and I love to hang out and binge-watch TV shows once we get our

---

[*] "The Right Balance," *Tabletalk*, February 2015.

daughters down for the night. While that is good "together time" for us, it does come at a price. We often wake up feeling unrested the next morning. And when I wake up and do not feel rested, I'm more likely to have a short temper with my wife and daughters and just be less alert and mentally available in general.

Maybe rest for you can be a twenty-minute power nap whether you're at work or home. I know napping is a bit counterintuitive to the way our society typically operates. Nonetheless, findings from research studies show that those who nap are less frustrated throughout the rest of their day than those who do not nap.[1]

And just a tidbit for those who cannot find rest because of working excessively long hours: a 2015 study found that fifty hours of work per week is the maximum most of us can work productively.[2] From hour fifty-one onward, we are virtually unproductive. In fact, in this study the author found that those who worked seventy hours per week were no more productive than those who worked fifty-five hours. That's fifteen hours of work with virtually no return for you (or your employer). So if taking a nap isn't an option, consider shortening your workday to get more sleep during the night by going to bed earlier or waking up a little later. Maybe start making a gradual change by getting more rest one or two nights per week.

If we don't take rest seriously, we'll hit a point when the only solution is a drastic change that could come with major consequences. This was the case with former megachurch pastor Pete Wilson, who resigned in September 2016 after fourteen years of leading his church. He said, "I really need your prayers and I need your support. We've said that this is a church where it's OK to not be OK, and I'm not OK. I'm tired. And I'm broken and I just need some rest."[3]

> **If we don't take rest seriously, we'll hit a point when the only solution is a drastic change that could come with major consequences.**

Now, I'm not casting Wilson in a negative light. In fact, I truly admire him for what he did. He is putting his family, his health, and his own spiritual well-being before his job. My point is that we should all seek rest on a regular basis so that we don't reach such an ultimate breaking point. Take this opportunity to think through how you can include more restful moments in your life. Maybe even put this book down and close your eyes for a few minutes.

Finances

> *The borrower becomes the lender's slave.*
> — Proverbs 22:7b

Thus far I haven't mentioned money too much in this book. However, what many people do not realize is that work-life *im*balance can often stem from a person's need or desire to make money. As Proverbs mentions, when we owe too much to a lender we effectively become his slave. And this often manifests itself in having to work too many hours to pay off our debts. Or, maybe we aren't actually in any major debt, but we just like to have really nice stuff. This desire for more stuff or nicer stuff can make us a slave to the job just as much as if we were in debt. In fact, a strong correlation exists between materialism and work-life *im*balance.[4]

So how do we get out from under the thumb of debt and materialism? Let me start by saying that I'm *not* a certified financial planner or money guru. However, a lot of great resources out there have helped my family and millions of others live a life in which we control the money instead of letting the money control us. A line from the Switchfoot song "If the House Burns Down Tonight" comes to mind: "You possess your possessions or they possess you?"[5] This is still a constant struggle in our society (and even for me) when we are bombarded daily with ads for the newest gadgets and hottest clothes.

If you're in debt, I encourage you to visit DaveRamsey.com and DavidBach.com to find more information about how to strategically approach your debt. While this does not serve as a formal endorsement of these two financial authors, both stress strategic approaches to getting out of debt. For those of us struggling with materialism, we need to hear the powerful words of Ecclesiastes 5:10: "He who loves money will not be satisfied with money, nor he who loves abundance with his income." This

95

is a call to shift our focus away from money to those with eternal value. Much like the advice I gave to workaholics in Chapter 5, I encourage those who are materialistic to seek guidance from a pastor or Christian counselor. Spending time with your family has much more eternal value than what you buy them.

> *Spending time with your family has much more eternal value than what you buy them.*

Spend less and go to bed early—that might be what some readers have just heard me say in this brief chapter. I promise I'm not trying to spoil your fun. However, if we can make small shifts in how we spend our money and in our sleep habits, it will pay big dividends in how we lead our families and perform at work.

Action Steps

- **Go to bed earlier**. I actually took my own advice. While I still love to binge-watch TV with my wife at night, I took the proactive step to go to bed twenty to thirty minutes earlier than I had been. It has made a world of difference in how I feel when I wake up each morning. It's also made me more effective with my exercise and time-management.

- **Rest.** Find rest in life's margins. We're all busy and we're all going to be tired from time-to-time. During your day, when can you find a few minutes of rest? If you have an office at work, can you close your door for fifteen to twenty minutes and close your eyes (if so, be sure to set yourself an alarm!)? If you stay at home with your kids, could you find a few minutes of rest during their naptime (or institute a twenty-minute "quiet time" policy if your kids no longer nap)?* Even if you can't take a nap, can you find a time and place to relax for a few minutes?

- **Evaluate your purchasing habits.** *Why am I buying that? Do I need that?* I'm just as tempted as anyone else to buy something because I feel it will make me look cool, etc. About a year ago I needed to purchase a car. I knew I wanted a car on the lower end of the pricing scale. However, I found myself looking at cars ten to fifteen thousand dollars more than the price I originally had in mind. Why? Because I thought driving that car would make me look cool (as if anyone cares!). Once I realized the motivation behind my car-browsing behavior, I refocused my search on a car *below* what I originally intended to pay. The lower price equaled a lower car payment, which fit into our family budget and didn't add a financial strain.

- **Budget your money.** Financial guru Dave Ramsey has famously said, "A budget is simply

---

* * When our oldest daughter was born I taught three days per week and my wife taught the other two. Each time Emily went down for a nap during my days at home with her, I would take a twenty- to thirty-minute nap too. If she slept for one hour, I was more efficient at grading papers for forty minutes *after* a twenty-minute nap than if I'd graded for the entire hour.

97

spending your money with intention."[6] My wife and I have had a budget for our income and expenses since we first got married. We reevaluate it each year to make adjustments. Our priority has been to stick with our budget and avoid debt (other than our home mortgage and reasonably priced cars). This prevents us from feeling like we have to work extra hours to make more money, allowing us to maintain a good work-life balance. While this chapter is not a financial roadmap for you to follow, many great budgeting tools exist, such as EveryDollar.com.

8

QIK GOALS

A goal properly set is halfway reached.[*]

If I've done an adequate job of writing this book, then hopefully you're excited about trying out one or more of the work-life balance strategies described within it. That's a good start. However, I want to draw from social science research one more time before you put this book down.

Many of us tend to make goals and plans but often fail to follow through with them completely. There could be multiple reasons for this phenomenon, but one of the biggest reasons our goals do not get achieved is because we do not think them through. In other words, when we haphazardly set goals, we tend *not* to reach those goals. On the other hand, over one thousand research studies lend support to the idea that properly setting goals is the key to actually achieving goals.[1]

---

[*] This quote has been attributed to both Abraham Lincoln and Zig Ziglar.

So how do we properly set our goals, and why does this help us reach them? Among other ways, properly setting goals focuses our energy in the right direction (i.e., toward the goal) and increases our persistence toward the goal.[2] While many goal-setting techniques exist, the QIK method has worked well for me:

Q = Quantifiable
I = Implementable
K = Known

This three-step method for setting your goals is straightforward, easy, and helpful for clarifying your goals.

The first step, *quantifiable*, helps us figure out how to measure our goal and provides a target. For instance, "I want to do a good job of getting new clients" isn't quantifiable. However, "I want to secure contracts with ten new clients," is easily quantifiable. In the first example, how do we know what a "good job" is? In the second example, we've placed a quantity on "good" so that we know where we're heading in terms of securing new clients.

> *Over one thousand research studies lend support to the idea that properly setting goals is the key to actually achieving them.*

The second step of the QIK method is to have *implementable* goals. That is, what action(s) can be taken to make sure progress is being made toward the goal? Another aspect of implementation is whether or not the goal can even be reached without taking drastic action. Perhaps you've set a quantifiable goal of exercising for twenty minutes each day, three times per week. That's great! But what can you do to provide more structure to your goal? What if you *implemented* a schedule where you exercised during your lunch break on Monday, Wednesday, and Friday each week? That provides more precision to your goal. Furthermore, for many of us, the notion of exercising three times per week is not so drastic that it cannot be implemented.

Finally, it's helpful if we make our goals *known*. You don't have to tell the whole world that you're planning to start exercising. You may even choose not to post that goal on social media. Instead, make your goal known to those who are going to assist you in meeting your goal (as opposed to those who may hinder your progress). This might be your spouse, a friend, or a coworker. Why should we make our goal known to others? An experiment conducted by Professor Gail Matthews found support for the idea of telling someone about your goal.[3] In her experiment, those who told someone about their goal were more likely to follow through and achieve their goal than those who didn't tell anyone.

How I've Used QIK

Prior to our second daughter's birth, I contacted our insurance agent to buy more life insurance. He asked about my height and weight. Upon giving him that information, he said my monthly premium would fall into the second tier, but if I lost eleven pounds I would qualify for the first-tier rate, which was their lowest possible monthly premium. It would save us approximately thirty dollars per month. He had me at "saving money." That was all I needed to get motivated.

I could have simply told myself, "I'm going to lose weight" and let that be the end of it. Instead, I used the QIK method to set my goal:

1) Quantifiable: I'm going to lose twelve pounds. (I wanted to lose slightly more than the agent said I needed to.)
2) Implementable: I will cut out carbs, go to the gym twice a week, and run twice a week. (Farewell, pizza and donuts.)
3) Known: I will tell my wife about my quantifiable, implementable, and ultimately money-saving goal. (She wholeheartedly approved.)

As you can see, my goal met all three facets of the QIK method. I had an exact number I wanted to reach, a way to implement actions to achieve my goal, and I made the goal known to my wife and a couple of other friends. Furthermore, the steps I took to implement this goal were not so extreme that I couldn't feasibly do it. Had I said I planned to cut my diet down to five hundred calories per day and daily run seventeen miles, I would have violated the *implementable* requirement. As it turns out, I lost the twelve pounds and got the cheapest rate available on life insurance. I got healthier in the process too.

The QIK method doesn't take long to use when setting your goal, but it can reap major benefits in terms of actually reaching your goal. My hope is that you'll try this method with one of the work-life balance strategies in this book. Start simple, but commit to making a change in order to improve your work-life balance.

CONCLUSION

If you stuck with me to the end, you now have a toolbox full of strategies that can help improve your work-life balance! Often, when we have work-life *im*balance we feel extremely overwhelmed and don't know what to do to fix it. Start by working on your spiritual well-being (Chapter 2) and then select one or two other strategies from this book to focus on (Chapters 3–8). Remember, the spiritual well-being chapter is a non-negotiable and must be the foundation for the rest of the strategies. When your heart's desires align with God's character and His plan for your life, then making any other necessary adjustments to find better work-life balance should happen more easily. As I mentioned in the introduction, God is in favor of work-life balance!

However, you may hear loud voices of opposition to your pursuit of work-life balance. Let God be your strength! Lean on the words of Isaiah 40:29: "He gives strength to the weary and increases the power of the weak."* Remember, investing in your spouse and

* NIV

children is one of the most important investments you can ever make (see Deuteronomy 6:6–7.) My prayer is that you find more time to invest in your family and feel less stressed by the everyday rush of life.

INVITATION

As you've been reading this book you may have been challenged by the truth that all of us have a crucial spiritual dynamic in our lives. Many people live, move, and breathe each day without considering the massive need that we have as human beings to be spiritually whole again. In fact, all throughout our lives, much of what we do is driven by our pursuit of something to fill the spiritual void within us. Money, work, sports, possessions, hobbies—all good resources, but all equally horrible substitutes for God.

You have been created uniquely with a personality, skill-set, background, and natural abilities that have formed the direction of your life.

The Bible communicates to us that our uniqueness is God's fingerprint upon us. Being formed in His image,* we have been fearfully and wonderfully made,†

---

* *Genesis 1:27 | God created man in His own image, in the image of God He created him; male and female He created them.*
† *Psalms 139:14 | I will give thanks to You, for I am fearfully and wonderfully made; Wonderful are Your works, And my soul knows it very well.*

to find our definition in His presence.‡ But there's just one problem: The sin that is present in our lives has cut us off from knowing Him, fellowshipping with Him, and finding our life's purpose from Him.§ Sin always separates and, for us, it has separated the most essential part of our humanity.

But God showed "His own love toward us, in that while we were yet sinners, Christ died for us" (Romans 5:8). God knew the degree of our separation and He used the depths of His strength to bridge the seemingly impassable gulf created by our sin. He sent Jesus, His one and only Son, to take our sin.** As we put our faith in His finished work we are restored to a relationship with the Father who loves us.††

Have you put your faith in Jesus? Today, even as you read these words, if you believe that your sin has separated you from Him, then respond by talking to Him. Tell Him that you know you are a sinner and that you trust in what Jesus has done to deliver you. Ask Him to free you from your sin and make Jesus the most treasured possession in your life.

If you have done this today, then because of Jesus, you have been set upon the path of life.‡‡ You have been set free from the dominion of sin and death so

---

‡ *Ephesians 2:10 | For we are His workmanship, created in Christ Jesus for good works, which God prepared beforehand so that we would walk in them.*

§ *Isaiah 59:2 | And your sins have hidden His face from you so that He does not hear.*

** *2 Corinthians 5:21 | He made Him who knew no sin to be sin on our behalf, so that we might become the righteousness of God in Him.*

†† *John 3:16 | For God so loved the world, that He gave His only begotten Son, that whoever believes in Him shall not perish, but have eternal life.*

‡‡ *Psalms 16:11 | You will make known to me the path of life; In Your presence is fullness of joy; In Your right hand there are pleasures forever.*

that you can discover your life's purpose in His presence.§§

I would encourage you that if you responded to this message through this book, please email me or Russell to share that good news and let us encourage you.

Ryan Johnson
ryan@madetoworship.net

---

§§ *Romans 8:1 | Therefore there is now no condemnation for those who are in Christ Jesus.*

NOTES

Introduction

1. Lydia Saad, "The '40-Hour' Workweek Is Actually Longer – by Seven Hours," *Gallup*, last modified August 29, 2014, http://www.gallup.com/poll/175286/hour-workweek-actually-longer-seven-hours.aspx.

2. V. S. Major, K. J. Klein, and M. G. Ehrhart, "Work Time, Work Interference with Family, and Psychological Distress," *Journal of Applied Psychology*, no. 87, (2002): 427–36.

Chapter 1: A Faith-Based Perspective for Work-Life Balance

1. Cliff Knight, e-mail communication to author, October 1, 2014.

Chapter 2: Spiritual Well-Being

1. Dennis and Barbara Rainey, "Defeating Selfishness in Your Marriage," *FamilyLife*, http://www.familylife.com/articles/topics/marriage/staying-married/resolving-conflict/defeating-selfishness-in-your-marriage.

Chapter 3: Exercise

1. "Exercise or Physical Activity," *National Center for Health Statistics*, http://www.cdc.gov/nchs/fastats/exercise.htm.

2. R. W. Clayton, C. Thomas, B. Singh, and D. Winkel, "Exercise as a Means of Reducing Perceptions of Work-Family Conflict: A Test of the Roles of Self-efficacy and Psychological Strain," *Human Resource Management*, no. 54, (2015): 1013–1035.

3. R. Clayton, "How Regular Exercise Helps You Balance Work and Family," *Harvard Business Review*, https://hbr.org/2014/01/how-regular-exercise-helps-you-balance-work-and-family.

4. Jeff Galloway, "Run Walk Run: It began in 1974," *Jeffgalloway.com*, http://www.jeffgalloway.com/training/run-walk.

5. "The Scientific 7-Minute Workout," Gretchen Reynolds, *New York Times*, last modified May 9, 2013, http://well.blogs.nytimes.com/2013/05/09/the-scientific-7-minute-workout.

Chapter 4: Emotional Intelligence

1. David Walton, *Introducing Emotional Intelligence: A Practical Guide* (London: Icon Books, 2013).

2. Darrin Patrick, "Integrity," *The Journey*, http://thejourney.org/media/walk/integrity.

3. John Calvin, *Institutes of the Christian Religion*.

4. *Emotional Intelligence as a Predictor of Work-Family Balance*. Presentation at the Annual Conference of the Society of Emotional Intelligence. Russell Clayton, Ph.D., October 23, 2015.

5. A. Carmeli, "The Relationship Between Emotional Intelligence and Work Attitudes, Behavior and Outcomes: An Examination among Senior Managers," *Journal of Managerial Psychology*, no. 18 (2003): 788–813.

6. L. N. Sharma, "Emotional Intelligence as a Correlate to Work Life Balance," *Global Journal of Finance and Management*, no. 6, (2014): 551–556.

7. Jessica Stillman, "3 Habits That Will Increase Your Empathy," *Inc.*, last modified August 22, 2014, http://www.inc.com/jessica-stillman/3-habits-that-will-increase-your-empathy.html.

Chapter 5: Time Management

1. Charles Stanley, *Success God's Way: Achieving True Contentment and Purpose* (Nashville: Thomas Nelson, 2002).
2. Tony Schwartz, "The Magic of Doing One Thing at a Time," *Harvard Business Review*, https://hbr.org/2012/03/the-magic-of-doing-one-thing-a.html.
3. J. S. Rubinstein, D. E. Meyer, and J. E. Evans, "Executive Control of Cognitive Processes in Task Switching," *Journal of Experimental Psychology: Human Perception and Performance*, no. 27, 4 (2001): 763–797.

Chapter 6: Career Management

1. A. Saltzman, *Downshifting: Reinventing Success on a Slower Track* (Perennial, 1992).
2. S. Behson, *The Working Dad's Survival Guide: How to Succeed at Work and at Home* (Melbourne, FL: Motivational Press, 2015).
3. Alyssa Newcomb, "Why MongoDB CEO Max Schireson Quit Because He Couldn't Have It All," *ABC News*, last modified August 6, 2014, http://abcnews.go.com/Technology/mongodb-ceo-max-schireson-quits-best-job-spend/story?id=24861491.

Chapter 7: Rest and Finances

1. J. R. Goldschmied et al., "Napping to Modulate Frustration and Impulsivity: A Pilot Study. *Personality and Individual Differences,* no. 86 (2015): 164–167.
2. J. Pencavel, "The Productivity of Working Hours," *The Economic Journal,* no. 125 (2015): 2052–2076.
3. "Megachurch Pastor Pete Wilson Is Resigning: 'I'm Not OK. I'm Tired. I'm Broken,'" *Relevant Magazine*, last modified September 12, 2016, http://www.relevantmagazine.com/slices/megachurch-pastor-pete-wilson-resigning-im-not-ok-im-tired-im-broken.
4. Switchfoot, "If the House Burns Down Tonight," *Where the Light Shines Through*, produced by Switchfoot and John Fields (San Diego, CA: Vanguard Records, 2016), Compact Disc.

5. M. D. Promislo, J. R. Deckop, R. A. Giacalone, and C. L. Jurkiewicz, "Valuing Money More than People: The Effects of Materialism on Work-Family Conflict," *Journal of Occupational and Organizational Psychology,* no. 83 (2010): 935–953.
6. "The Truth About Budgeting," *Dave Ramsey,* https://www.daveramsey.com/blog/the-truth-about-budgeting.

Chapter 8: QIK Goals

1. T. R. Mitchell and D. Daniels, "Motivation," *Comprehensive Handbook of Psychology: Industrial Organizational Psychology Vol. 12,* eds. W. C. Borman, D. R. Ilgen, and R. J. Klimoski (New York, NY: Wiley, 2003): 225–254.
2. E. A. Locke and G. P. Latham, "Building a Practically Useful Theory of Goal Setting and Task Motivation: A 35-year Odyssey," *American Psychologist,* no. 57 (2002): 705–717.
3. "Study Focuses on Strategies for Achieving Goals, Resolutions," Dominican University of California, http://www.dominican.edu/dominicannews/study-highlights-strategies-for-achieving-goals.

ABOUT THE AUTHOR

Russell Clayton is a college professor, author, and speaker, but his favorite roles are husband and father. Russell and his wife Alicia live in Tampa Bay, FL, with their two daughters and miniature dachshund Charlie. They enjoy frequent visits to Disney World and other fun spots in the central Florida area.

Russell has been a college professor for over five years, and prior to that enjoyed a successful career in fundraising. He graduated from Auburn University in 2000 with B.S. in Business Administration and worked for seven years before returning to school at the University of Mississippi to earn his Ph.D. in Business Administration.

He is a thought-leader on the soft-side of management, including work-life balance, emotional intelligence, and leadership. Russell has published his research in several peer-reviewed academic journals including *Journal of Vocational Behavior*, *Human Resource Management*, *Human Relations*, and *The Journal of Leadership & Organizational Studies*. In addition, he has written for and/or been quoted in such popular press outlets as *Harvard Business Review*, *USA Today*, *Fast Space Company*, *INC.*, *CNBC*, *Huffington Post*, *NBC News*, and *Runner's World*.

To stay in touch with Russell or to learn more about having him speak to your group, visit www.russellclayton.net.

82763319R00071

Made in the USA
Columbia, SC
05 December 2017